AF326779

Behavioral Tells:

Read the Hidden Signals Behind Every Action. What People Reveal Without Saying a Word.

By Patrick King
Social Interaction and Conversation Coach at
www.PatrickKingConsulting.com

Table of Contents

Section 1

Chapter 1: What Stops Us from Accurately Perceiving Others?

The first step to really reading a person?

Pay attention!

You'd be surprised how much you can see if you only *look*.

Most of us don't see what's right in front of us for one simple reason: there is something in the way of our perception.

"Perceptual barriers" interfere with our accurate perception of others. This seems obvious, but it's a point worth laboring—if you only perceive what you want to perceive, it's as good as not perceiving at all.

➜ **Key insight: If you can remove bias, expectation, assumption, ego, prejudice, interpretation, judgment—in short, as much of your subjectivity as possible—then you can master the art of reading people.**

Here are some of the things you may not realize are undermining your ability to really understand other people.

<u>*Perceptual Selectivity*</u>

Simply, this is the tendency to choose certain objects from the environment while ignoring others.

How do people decide what to focus on? It all depends on their:

- Beliefs
- Values
- Needs
- Attitudes
- Interests
- Background

Perception is selective, but it's usually *not* determined by the stimulus itself, but by what we're bringing to that stimulus.

To really see what is in front of them, a person must screen out most stimuli and focus on only a few.

How do they do that?

That's what makes all the difference.

Importantly, being selective is not a huge problem—we all do it. Rather, we need to be aware of when it's happening so we don't confuse our own conclusions with reality.

Example: You're in an ambiguous situation. Someone is suddenly upset. You think, "Must be that time of the month," and congratulate yourself for being great at reading between the lines.

See the problem?

Your selective focus on one aspect of the situation (the person being female), combined with your own beliefs and assumptions, has led you to make a guess about someone that is probably... distorted.

It's more accurate to say that you have perceived your own intellectual shortcuts rather than something objectively in your environment.

Attribution

Attribution is what we do when we try to explain why people behave as they do.

Example: You see a child having a tantrum. You think, "He's deliberately trying to push my buttons."

- This is not a perception of behavior.
- This is a *guess as to the cause and motivation* of a perceived behavior.

Big difference!

It's normal to draw conclusions about the factors that influence people or to try to make meaning of their behavior. We all like to feel that the world makes a certain sense and that we can reliably predict the behavior of others. But again, in this way, our own bias may creep in and obscure what is actually happening.

We are so busy seeing what we *think* is there, that we can't see what actually *is* there!

> **Example:** You're talking to a person from Japan. They've made a mistake. You've brought it to their attention, and now they're grinning at you and nodding furiously.

How would you explain this behavior?

Well, if you did this yourself, it would mean one thing only: You didn't take the situation seriously and were even laughing rudely at the other person.

- You ask yourself the question, "Why are they behaving this way?"
- You answer the question as though you were answering for *yourself*: "Because they don't take this seriously."
- The reality? It's just a cultural difference. The Japanese often smile in awkward situations in order to defuse tension—it is the opposite of rudeness!

Attribution errors can *seem like* perception... but often they just get in the way.

Stereotyping

Stereotyping is judging someone based on what you think about the group to which they belong.

It's a basic human trait.

A kind of cognitive shortcut.

We see a person as part of a single group or class, then give that person positive or negative traits based on what most people think about that group as a whole.

It's one of the ways we simplify our world and make it easier to understand. It's also a surefire way to distort our perception of how people actually are— they're usually a lot more complex than stereotypes would suggest.

Have you ever been really surprised to learn that a person you thought you knew was actually quite different from what you first thought? It's a great opportunity to ask *why* your expectations were so subverted.

➜ **Important: Stereotypes don't have to be full-blown prejudices to distort perception.**

In fact, our perception can be most disturbed by those assumptions we have that are usually true.

Example: A drug-trafficking operation could work precisely because it employs the help of unassuming elderly women to transport packages. The stereotype that little old ladies don't smuggle heroin is pretty accurate—but believing it will allow you to miss the truth.

Stereotypes distort perception—but only if we don't know they're there.

The Halo Effect

Speaking of little old ladies, **the "halo effect" is the tendency to judge people based on a single trait, whether that trait is good or bad**.

The halo effect is very similar to stereotyping. However, in stereotyping, a person is judged by the group they belong to, while with the halo effect, they are judged by a single trait they possess.

We sometimes judge a person based on the first thing we see or hear about them.

- If someone is kind, we may automatically see them as trustworthy, competent, hardworking, and so on.
- If someone is beautiful, we might wrongly assume that they are also healthy or intelligent.
- If they're financially successful, we might decide that they're also experts in other areas, like politics, economics, or social issues.

In real life and with real people, these traits sometimes go together, and sometimes they don't. A celebrity may have something relevant to share about animal rights or the best diet for children, but they may also be just as ignorant as the next person.

By the same token, there is nothing to say that a doctor who goes to prison for assault suddenly knows any *less* about medicine than he did before (let's call it a "devil horns" effect!) or that people who are color blind can't be good artists.

In either case, if we take one observation and *over-extrapolate* it, we stop accurately perceiving what is actually in front of us.

Projection

Sometimes, we perceive not what somebody is, but what *we* are—we project onto them the same way a film projector puts its image onto a screen. This idea originally comes from the theories of Carl Jung, who explained how people might disidentify with some unwanted traits, and then seem to discover them in other people.

But projection doesn't have to be a serious psychological phenomenon involving shadows and unconscious material. Sometimes it simply occurs because **people lazily assume that others are more like themselves than they really are**.

> **Example:** Have you ever been surprised to find that someone you knew had very different religious or political opinions than you originally believed? You might have enjoyed their company and simply assumed that they had the same beliefs as you, just to be surprised when you wrongly assume their response to something. Or, perhaps you observed some behavior in them and

automatically concluded that their reason for acting that way must be the same as your own.

Skilled people readers know how to read other people—not images of themselves projected onto other people.

<u>Perceptual Set</u>

A perceptual set is a set of beliefs about how others see and understand certain situations.

> **Example:** A manager may come to believe and act as if his workers are lazy and just want to get as much as they can from the organization without giving their best.

This is a perceptual *set*. It's a mix of different:

- Assumptions
- Preconceptions
- Ideas

A perceptual set is like a lens or filter laid over reality, or a set of repeated stories and expectations. Instead of perceiving a person directly, we just consult the perceptual set that tells us exactly who they are.

> **Example:** A family has a perceptual set for one child that includes a whole narrative about them being special, unique, and precious, while the perceptual set for the other child revolves around their being difficult and troubled.

Want to know how you can tell a perceptual set is at work? Notice when people distort a neutral stimulus so that it fits the set, rather than changing the set.

For example, the "black sheep" described in the family above may often behave in intelligent, kind, and unexpected ways, but this behavior will be interpreted so that it *always supports the pre-existing perceptual set.*

How?

The parents might perceive this behavior, but say, "Oh, every once in a while, he does stunts like this just to show off. He's always been egotistical like that. He's just looking for attention, as usual."

Implicit Personality Theory

When judging and making assumptions about other people, a person's thoughts are affected by **how he thinks certain human traits are linked to each other**.

This is something you might never have given a second thought—but can you be sure that the "rules" you assume control the way personality traits cluster are actually accurate?

Later, we'll see that personality theories have been a perennial fascination for social theorists, psychologists, and lay people-readers since time began. But an *implicit* personality theory is a private, inner model of what personalities are and how they are formed.

Here, *implicit* means a theory that's:

- Unexamined
- Unconscious
- (Usually) inaccurate

Example: Hard work is often linked to being honest. People usually think that anyone who works hard must also be honest.

Have *you* ever made this implicit association?

If someone told you that someone at work had been stealing petty cash, wouldn't you tend to suspect the lazier members of the team over the workaholics and "Type A" people?

It's because you're working with an *implicit personality model* that assumes those traits go together.

But if you examine this association, you'll see that there's no reason to think that one implies the other. If you don't believe it's possible for someone to share *both* traits, or neither, then you stop being able to accurately perceive that person when they cross your path.

Expectancy

Expectation is the tendency to see people, things, and events based on how we thought they would be in the first place.

> **Example:** Imagine you're about to be introduced to someone you are told is a priest. You know very little about priests and have no experience with them, but you can't help expecting certain things from the interaction.

Without realizing it, you automatically anticipate that this person must be:

- Stern
- Upright
- Softly spoken
- Middle-aged
- Kind of boring and maybe a bit of a killjoy
- Morally superior
- Compassionate
- Perhaps hiding a terrible secret or two…?

When you actually meet the priest, your expectations mean you are *unconsciously looking for confirmation* of all the above.

- You discount all the things that don't line up with the picture you already have in your head.
- And the things that *do* line up? You focus on and amplify them.

Magically, this priest seems to be… exactly what you thought they'd be.

You can see why this is sometimes also called a "self-fulfilling prophecy"!

Let's say you believe that priests are all compassionate and non-judgmental. When you meet, you start confessing all your personal troubles. The priest sees that you need his attention and politely gives it. You think, "See? Priests are compassionate."

However, if you *hadn't* led the priest down that path by confessing so much, you might have discovered that he would have preferred to talk about Formula One racing.

You are no longer seeing the priest as he is, but as you expect him to be.

Perceptual Defense

One final thing to consider: **We may not be able to accurately perceive people simply because it's too threatening to fully acknowledge what they are, or what they are saying.**

Here, "threatening" can encompass a broad range of ideas:

- It can mean subtle but culturally unacceptable ideas that your mind unconsciously chooses not to see.
- It can mean ignoring things you're not ready to deal with on a personal level.

- It can mean downplaying or minimizing the size of an idea that just plain hurts to think about.

    Example: Have you ever noticed that some people can be very obviously gay, and yet many people around them seem oblivious to the fact? Their eyes work; it's just that they don't really want to see!

It can go the other way, too.

    Example: If someone is very anxious and suspicious, anything their partner does may be perceived as strange and troubling.

In the first example, the defense is not to perceive fully; in the second example, the defense is to see things that aren't actually there—so they can protect themselves.

In both cases, the perception is not accurate.

A little perceptual defense is only human, and sometimes it's necessary. After all, we don't tell little kids that it's impossible for them to become astronauts—a little modification of a harsh truth is sometimes necessary!

But we need to be alert to where *perception* is giving way to *protection*.

<u>*Improving Your Perceptual Accuracy*</u>

As you can see, one thing consistently gets in the way of accurate perception: ourselves!

All of the above share something in common: The error of prioritizing our *idea* about reality over reality itself.

Anytime we do this, we undermine our powers of perception.

So how do we get better?

Know thyself.

Knowing who you are is a powerful way to avoid perceptual distortions. It lets you clarify:

- What is *your* stuff?
- What is *their* stuff?
- What values, beliefs, and blind spots do you bring to the table?

To be a good people-reader, you don't have to completely remove these blind spots, you just need to be honest about the fact that they are there.

➜ **Important: Overwhelmingly, people usually see others wrong because they don't see *themselves* right.**

The better a person knows himself, the better he can understand other people.

Importantly, don't just flesh out your idea of who you *want* to be, or focus only on the good. Instead, be clear about all that other stuff, too:

- Your prejudices.
- Your fears.
- Your bad habits.

A good question to ask yourself is: "What are my most recurrent personal biases and prejudices?"

If you say "none," then there is work to do!

We all have them.

Know what yours are.

> **Example:** If you are aware that you tend to assume that everyone is less intelligent than you are, be honest about how this skews your perception. What can you routinely do to offset this tendency?

Cultivate empathy.

We tend to think of empathy and kindness as more or less the same thing.

But empathy has two components:

- Perceptual
- Cognitive

Empathy means not merely caring about how others feel, but actually understanding it and being able to perceive it. After all, how can you care and be kind if you don't even know what is happening, or why?

Empathy is a natural trait, but it's also a skill one can develop over time with the help of a good feedback system and genuine interactions with others.

Don't simply assume you are already empathetic enough. Constantly check that your perceptions about others are actually true—or else you risk becoming one of those people who crows about being an "empath" but who really, really isn't!

→ Get into the habit of *asking, not assuming.*

Example: If you're worried one day that you've offended someone, don't just take it as a given that you have. Don't just assume that your guess about their inner perception is 100 percent accurate. Confirm your reading of the situation by asking them.

Empathy is not all about mind-reading—sometimes good old-fashioned communication leads to far more understanding!

Be positive.

Perceptions are affected by how people feel.

- When we have a bad opinion of someone or something, our view of that person or thing will be skewed.
- If we have a bad opinion of *ourselves* or of life in general, that cannot help but color the way we see the person in front of us.

"Positive" here doesn't mean wearing rose-colored glasses.

It means cultivating an attitude that is secure enough to allow us to set aside our own preferences so we can more clearly see the way things really are.

This attitude is:

- Gentle
- Curious
- Flexible
- Open-minded
- Receptive

It's the mindset of, "Hm, here is a new person I know nothing about. I wonder what I'm going to learn about them?"

A good habit to practice: When dealing with someone you find difficult, routinely ask yourself, "What is working right now?"

This will train you to see possibility, options, solutions, and avenues you hadn't considered.

Be willing to learn.

If someone says something that seems totally wrong, ask what is right about it... and assume there *is* something.

- Ask how their perspective is enriching you.
- Ask what you can learn from any differences between you.

- Ask what that potential friction could be showing you about your own limitations.

Positivity → more accurate perception.

Postpone impression formation.

People have a natural tendency to quickly form strong opinions about things or people.

Just from one or two meetings, we can figure out what someone is like. Though this is an understandable part of human nature, we often sacrifice accuracy for speed and ease.

Remind yourself: It's annoying to be pigeon-holed by others based on just one or two of your traits, right?

Commit to not doing that to others.

➡ **Key Insight: Deliberately make the effort to just *wait*—you don't have to form an opinion about everything!**

Let people show you who they are.

That takes time.

➡ A great habit to cultivate: Change statements to questions.

Questions keep you curious and open-minded.

Questions keep you alert and receptive.

Questions improve your perception.

The moment you form a conclusion about someone, your perception is out of the game and you go into *assumption* mode instead!

> **Example:** You notice yourself wanting to say, "She's a snob." Instead, you turn it into a question. "Is she a snob?"

This simple shift allows you to notice the possibility that you could interpret her behavior in some other way.

It helps you notice what is happening, rather than you focusing on your premature *theory* about what is happening.

Practice open communication.

Many misunderstandings are caused by poor or one-way communication. Or, let's be honest, a complete lack of communication. A whole world of perceptual distortions can appear in a conversation if we are not conscious of how we send and receive information.

One good idea: Stop asking leading questions. Instead, ask with a genuinely open and curious mind and truly listen to what you're told. Imagine that you are not asking questions to confirm or disprove a running hypothesis, but are genuinely wanting to learn something... and perhaps even be surprised.

- You notice that someone insists on wearing cashmere, wool, and silk.

- "She's a snob" → "Is she a snob?"
- You ask her to tell you more about why she does this.
- You learn that she's not a snob at all, but has a skin allergy that makes wearing synthetic fabrics impossible.

Verify your perceptions by comparing them with others.

One way to reduce perceptual errors is to compare how you see something to how someone else sees it. You may have already done this in the past and been shocked at the discrepancy! By talking about how we see things, we learn about different points of view and may be able to understand the situation much better.

That said, comparing our perceptions with others doesn't mean they're right and we're wrong; rather, it's an exercise in perspective taking. In the same way that certain colors tend to change depending on what colors they appear next to, comparison can bring to light certain assumptions we didn't know we were making.

Chapter 2: The Art of Perspective Taking

Perspective taking is the ability to imagine another person's psychological viewpoint.

Perspective taking is not an ability we are innately capable of—it is a skill that needs to be learned like any other. It requires stepping outside of one's self-centeredness to genuinely see things from another's perspective. Not to see that person's situation through your own eyes, but see their situation as *they* would see it, through their eyes.

Empathy is about imagining what a person...

- Perceives
- Thinks
- Feels

... as themselves.

Perspective taking naturally leads to imagining what another person would *do*.

We can better predict their behavior because we more thoroughly understand their motivations.

"Theory of mind" is the ability to imagine someone else's mental state, even if it differs from our own.

> **Example:** The fashion designer Oscar de la Renta is said to have once advised women: "Walk like there are three men walking behind you."

Pause here to consider your perspective on his statement.

From his point of view, he imagined what it was like to be a woman and concluded that if there were three men walking behind you, you would probably walk in a sexier way.

But women were confused. If three men were walking behind them, they said, they might not be feeling sexy at all, but cautious and alert. They'd walk faster or even cross to the other side of the road.

Perspective matters.

And it's what Oscar de la Renta *lacked* in this case.

This story nicely illustrates a kind of perceptual blind spot:

- He was not imagining what it would be like to be a woman.
- He was imagining what it would be like for him, as a man, to be a woman.

Big difference!

Perhaps he had seen women in the street, thought they were sexy, then concluded that this experience of them as sexy was identical to what *they* were experiencing.

His perception was distorted.

He was unable to genuinely abandon his perspective and take up another.

Everybody *thinks* they have empathy.

Everybody thinks they can perspective-switch and find true understanding,

The truth? Few do.

The irony is that our insistence that we can switch perspectives properly is what actually prevents us from doing so!

Below are some ways to sincerely practice walking in another person's shoes—and not in the way that Oscar de la Renta does!

Tip 1: Watch a movie or TV show

Getting into movies or TV shows is a great way to learn how to see things from other people's points of view. Many believe reading fiction helps you really get into other people's feelings and see events from their points of view, but the same thing can be done with film—you are literally forced to take a certain angle on a situation.

When you want to see something from someone else's point of view, pick a movie or TV show and choose a character's point of view. You can even begin with a character who reminds you of yourself. As you get better at putting yourself in other people's shoes, try to ask yourself certain questions as you watch:

- What are they thinking, and why?
- Why are they behaving as they are?
- What are they trying to achieve?
- What emotions are they experiencing, and why?
- How are they explaining the situation to themselves?
- What aspects of the situation are most salient for them?

One of the problems with studying people this way is that it can be tricky to know if you've missed the mark or not. But a few questions can help you assess your reading:

- Were you able to understand the events on screen in a deeper way? In other words, could you more easily predict the ending or understand the character's choices? Did you feel like the story and the character "made sense"?
- Could you clearly see and articulate the reasons the character did what he or she did?

- Could you feel the emotions the character portrayed and point to where they came from?

Another problem is that not all film and TV is created equal. Practice this often enough and you may find your tastes changing because you more frequently spot a poorly developed character!

Tip 2: Use your (social) imagination

Imagining hypothetical situations is another good way to think about things from different points of view. The key is to really inject yourself into different roles and fully inhabit them.

You know how little children play with dolls, alternatively speaking for each one? You'll be practicing a similar exercise to develop your social imagination.

Here's how:

- Find a picture of people engaging in a dynamic scene—look at magazines, photos, movie stills, etc. You can also easily find pictures online.
- Look closely at the image and try to imagine a dramatic story to accompany it.
- Ask yourself:
  o What happened before the moment in the image?
  o What will come after?
  o What's going on?
  o How do each of the people feel about it?

Example: In your picture is a group of people, one of them holding a gun.

You ask yourself how they *feel* and try to really imagine being them in that moment.

- Are they scared? Angry?
- How do they see the other people in this moment?
- What are they focusing on most in the scene?
- Where is their attention going?
- What are they trying to achieve, and how?

Now, switch and inhabit the point of view of another person in the image, perhaps someone who has the gun pointed at them.

- How does their perspective compare?
- What do they think of the person with the gun?
- Where is their attention going and why?

As you can see, there are many layers to this—not just comprehending other people's emotions, but their attention, motivation, assessment of the emotions of other people around them, and so on.

We'll explore this in more depth in the next chapter.

Tip 3: Switch perspectives in your own life

Take a moment to recall a recent misunderstanding, argument, or conflict.

In the same way as you did above, try to hold a snapshot of this situation in your mind's eye, then deliberately switch between points of view, almost like you were changing radio stations.

What does the problem look like from the other person's perspective?

How do *you* appear to *them*?

If you're finding this exercise difficult, don't worry— it *is* difficult! Try answering these questions to deepen your insight:

- What has objectively happened?
- What has each person focused on in this situation?
- What is everyone's motivation?
- How do you think everyone feels?
- How is each person making sense of what is going on? How do they explain it?
- What do they think about *your* role? Is it accurate?
- How does each person frame the issue?

Though perspective taking is great for improving communication and helping smooth over conflict, it can be applied to improving our people-reading skills, too. The idea is that if we can fully understand *how a person sees things*, we understand more about them on a fundamental level.

The reverse is true, also—if we know who they are, we can more accurately understand how things will appear to them.

Chapter 3: The Four Personality Types and "Perceptual Positions"

When trying to read and analyze people, the human tendency is towards a kind of laziness:

- How can I simplify this?
- What "kind" of person am I looking at?
- What category do they belong to?

Though lazy, there is real value in such shortcuts.

- Centuries ago, in medieval times, people spoke about how the "humors" of the body determine personality (some people could be "choleric" or "sanguine," etc., according to the functions of their dominant organs).
- In Ayurveda, a person's physiological constitution is supposed to tell you a lot about their attitude, intelligence, and emotions.
- More recently, the Myers-Briggs Type Indicator (MBTI) and the Enneagram have become the personality assessment frameworks that capture the modern desire to put people in categories.

To this day, people continue to be captivated by the idea of what makes each of us unique—by putting us in groups with others who are similar!

We seem to be interested in where our psychological traits come from and how they're grouped, not just so we understand others better, but so we can better understand ourselves.

Typically, some fundamental human characteristics are identified and then combined in a matrix that yields a limited set of possible types.

One notable personality theory to understand is what's called the Big Five, or the OCEAN model.

This is a long-standing, well-researched framework in personality assessment that is used by psychologists the world over.

A person can score high or low on each of these main factors:

- **Openness** – Your natural curiosity and readiness to learn and experience new things.
- **Conscientiousness** – How thoughtful, considerate, or dependable you are.
- **Extraversion** – How outgoing, sociable, and assertive you are in social situations.
- **Agreeableness** – Your willingness to be sympathetic, accommodating, and cooperative with other people, and your broad concern/sympathy for them.
- **Neuroticism** – Your emotional style and the likeliness of emotional instability, mood

swings, depression, loneliness, anger, or sadness.

Whichever model you use, though, the idea is that if you know a person's *type*, you immediately have deeper insight into what makes them tick.

It's worth remembering that personality theories and frameworks of this kind are just that—models.

And models are necessarily *limited*.

In 2018, Northwestern University's Luis Amaral and colleagues conducted a worldwide survey. The researchers looked at the data of more than 1.5 million people who'd taken part in personality tests and started plotting where they scored on each of the Big Five factors.

Examining the patterns in their data, they managed to identify four main personality types (the most recurrent patterns of scoring on the Big Five factors): **"average," "reserved," "self-centered," and "role model."**

Their proposed personality types look like this:

Average
- The most common personality type.
- High scores in both neuroticism and extraversion—these people tend to be more sociable and assertive, but also fairly pessimistic and oversensitive.

- Low scores in openness—they're likely to be more routine-based, suspicious, conventional, and less open to abstraction.
- These people tend to seek attention but are not overly intellectually curious.
- More likely to be women.

Reserved
- Higher scores of agreeableness and conscientiousness—these are people who tend to be more trusting, sensitive, well-liked, and reliable.
- Lower scores for both openness and neuroticism—this means they are not as open-minded and curious, but once on a path, they stay the course with confidence and reliability.
- Low neuroticism also means they're more emotionally stable and get on well with others.
- Somewhat extroverted, but not overly so.

Role Models
- High scores in extraversion, openness, agreeableness, and conscientiousness—these are the people who tend to exhibit qualities that evoke respect and admired leadership, and which allow them to cultivate good relationships with others.
- Low scores in neuroticism—they are fairly confident and brave, taking calculated risks.
- High conscientiousness and openness means they are dependable and open to new ideas.
- They tend to be strong leaders.
- More likely to be women.

Self-Centered

- High scores in extraversion—such personalities are often very socially confident, energetic, and outgoing.
- Low scores in openness, agreeableness, and conscientiousness—so they may be impulsive, headstrong, bad-tempered, rude/insensitive, and fixed to their routines.
- Typically exhibit a self-serving attitude at the expense of others.

The findings for the above four groups were published in the journal *Nature Human Behavior*. The researchers' claim was that the four types clustered predictably in the way they ranked the five different OCEAN traits.

That means that the data consistently suggested that there were four recurrent ways in which people scored on the different aspects—rather than it being completely random.

So, what does that mean for the person who wants to master their people-reading skills?

Well, simple: It means that your job suddenly got a whole lot easier!

Example: You meet someone for the first time, and you notice a few things about them:

- She's a woman.
- She mentions interacting with her family and friends a lot (i.e., seems close to them and therefore pretty sociable and extroverted) but

always in the context of some sort of drama or dilemma (i.e., pretty high on neuroticism, too).

- When you mention something she says she's never heard about before, you notice that she shows no subsequent interest in it, preferring to steer the conversation back to familiar things instead of asking questions (i.e., low openness).
- She makes a little joke about pretending to be ill to get out of work (i.e., potentially low or average on conscientiousness).

Now, if you looked at all the above clues and came to the conclusion that you were dealing with an "average" personality type, would it be guaranteed that you were correct?

Of course not.

But as the evidence mounts, your hypothesis certainly becomes stronger. You may be dealing with the sort of person who has a rare blend of scores on each of the five traits. But it's not *likely*.

The researchers who proposed these four personality types were making probability claims—they used computational methods to analyze the data of 1.5 million people, and they found stable trends. That means that their findings can help you identify the most *likely* outcome—but never with 100% accuracy.

These four personality types are not foolproof, but they're a great starting point.

If you identify one, you can always use that as your "working model" and continue to observe in order to learn more about the person in front of you.

If this woman suddenly tells you that she used to be a UN goodwill ambassador and that she founded her own charity, you might adjust your assessment and look for further clues that she is actually closer to the "role model" type.

As you read and observe people, you are not just coming to conclusions and piecing clues together.

You are also eliminating possibilities.

Consider another example:

The researchers claim that teenage boys tend to be more highly represented in the "self-centered" category, and less so in the "role model" category. If one day you meet a teenage boy who is extremely low in agreeableness, then you can find out more about who he is by seeing who he *isn't*:

- Being low in agreeableness rules out the "role model" and "reserved" categories, leaving only "average" or "self-centered."
- Let's say that, due to him being a teenage boy, you *temporarily* assume he is in the "self-centered" category.

    But this is only temporary—when you get more data, you can rule out either one and be left with the most likely category.

You could still be completely wrong.

But you are probably closer to the truth!

The researchers for this study also point out that even though they've identified some stable patterns in personality clusters, this doesn't mean that personality itself is static and never changes over the course of human development.

- The teenager above may find that puberty makes him temporarily less agreeable and conscientious, and his youth may make him more extroverted and energetic.
- But what about in twenty years' time? He may morph into an enviable "role model" type.
- Likewise, he may be far more neurotic at school, but less so at home, where he is more comfortable.

➜ His personality didn't change, exactly; it just shifted a little given the change in environment.

Finally, a person may enhance or downplay certain aspects of their character simply because they are in our company. We can all imagine that a teenage boy would find himself being a little more agreeable and conscientious if he was in the company of a girl he had a crush on and wanted to impress!

We don't need to worry too much about this, however. All we can ever do is perceive the information in front of us in whatever moment we find ourselves in. The next time you are trying to read and understand a person from scratch, ask yourself a few of the following questions to narrow things down a bit:

- Are they generally high in everything except openness? They're probably **average**.
- If they're high in everything, low in openness but don't seem to be neurotic—they're probably **reserved**.
- Do they seem not very open-minded but neither extroverted nor introverted? Again, **reserved**—don't let the ordinary meaning of "reserved" fool you!
- Do they appear high in everything but unusually calm, content, and stable emotionally? A clear sign that they are a **role model**.
- Do they seem low in everything except extraversion? They're probably **self-centered**.
- Do they seem kind of average in everything? They might be **reserved** (*not* average, which scores quite high on most traits).
- Do they seem kind of volatile and emotional (awkward, cynical, fearful, unconfident, insecure, and defensive)? They're probably **average** (interesting, isn't it, that high scores on neuroticism are actually most common?).
- Not extroverted? They're likely **reserved**—the only ones who consistently score low on extraversion.
- Are they open-minded and willing to experience new things? They're **role models**—again, the only category that consistently scores high on this trait. If you see it, it's a sure sign you're talking to a role model.

One final word on these traits: Despite the impression the categories may give, there are no strict "good" traits or "bad" traits.

It's a question of *degree*, and of how a trait *functions*.

Consider:

- If you are *too* agreeable, you might find yourself being a bit of a doormat, a people-pleaser, or having poor boundaries. Being too open to experience may make you a little naïve and open for deception and manipulation.
- Similarly, being *too* conscientious can lead to stress, guilt, or weird codependent dynamics with others (i.e., those who are too low in conscientiousness!).
- Being overly neurotic isn't great, but a little neuroticism is useful if it allows us to properly assess risk, speak our truth, and assert our healthy boundaries. Too little neuroticism and we may lose our edge!

But there's another reason it's important to remember not to make value judgments when we observe and read others: We risk distorting our perception.

Example: If we personally think that extroverts are kind of annoying and superficial, we might notice this in someone and develop a perceptual set, stereotype, or expectation about them that colors everything else we perceive. If we have an unconscious preference for introversion or think that this is the "right" way to be, then we are jeopardizing our people-reading accuracy.

<u>*Perceptual Positions*</u>

Let's see if we can combine what we know about personality types with what we know about perspective taking.

The perceptual positions framework is a basic method for understanding another person's viewpoint.

Perceptual positions are a form of modeling that allows us to step into somebody else's shoes...

- To see what they see.
- To hear what they hear.
- To feel what they feel.

The technique comes from NLP—neurolinguistic programing—and has plenty of uses, including:

- defusing conflict,
- fostering empathy,
- learning more about yourself,
- communicating well, and
- reading and analyzing people more effectively.

If we combine it with a good personality theory, we can rapidly learn a lot about a person.

There are three perceptual positions: the first, the second, and the third (also called the observer or meta-position).

Your task is to analyze or read a situation *from these three different positions.*

Doing so gives you much more information (and empathy) and brings extra dimension to the entire encounter.

➔   **Important:** You are not just "thinking about" things when in any position—you are engaging *all* of your senses.

Let's look more closely.

First Position

➔   **This is like the "I" frame.**

It's the world as you see it through your own perceptual lens—a natural place to start.

To flesh out this position, consider your perceptions on all five senses and become fully associated and embodied here. You'd be surprised at just how much you can learn about others in a situation when you more clearly understand where *you* are in the interaction.

Second Position

➔   **Also thought of as "the other" position.**

It's the ability to see the same situation that is seen by the person in the first position, but through *their* personal filters.

Remember: Do this *as them*—not as yourself imagining them. There's a big difference! If you were talking to a child, for example, and you were taking the second position and imagining their perception, literally picture what it would be like to be small and look up at a taller adult—you.

This is a natural place to be for therapists and coaches, but also salespeople and those trying to persuade or motivate.

Here, we are imagining someone else's perceptions.

Third Position

➔ **This is where we see the world through the "observer" filter.**

We are like a fly on the wall, observing the interaction from the outside.

- We are objective.
- We pass no judgment.

This position is not actually involved in the unfolding story, meaning it is a bigger and more neutral perspective. .

Now, all this may seem pretty abstract until it's put into context, so let's look at an example to show exactly how this model can be applied.

Example: You and your younger brother had a pretty significant disagreement recently. You want to make amends, so you invite him to stay at your place over the weekend for some brother-bonding time. When he shows up, he's brought a friend of his without asking you. To top it off, you hardly know this friend, and you aren't particularly fond of him. Now things are awkward.

Step 1

Goal: Occupy first position.

- Think about the situation, problem, or conversation.
- Consider this situation *from your own point of view.*
- Flesh out your perspective and associate with it fully, on all five senses.
- Try to describe the experience in one word or short phrase.

You begin by fully inhabiting your own perspective: You are feeling bad for the earlier argument, and genuinely want to smooth things over, but this unexpected intrusion is upsetting. Now you also feel an obligation to play host, which means you won't be able to relax and be as comfortable as you hoped. Not to mention, if he's there, you'll have to make amends with an audience who wasn't involved in the issue in the first place.

It's a lot to try and put into a single word, but if you had to condense it, you would say that **you feel taken advantage of**.

Step 2

Goal: Explore second position.

- Now look at the very same situation but from someone else's viewpoint.
- Describe this experience in a single word or short phrase, too.

You choose to look at the situation through your brother's point of view, as well as his friend's. You do this as fully and genuinely as you can. Let's take a look:

- In your brother's shoes, you're feeling worried. You know that you were in the right, and that your brother said he wanted to fix things. But the argument was pretty bad, and what if you say something and unintentionally start another disagreement? You're feeling anxious and could use the backup.
- You also know your brother is great with everyone. He enjoys having friends over and hanging out with people. Your friend is a great guy, surely your brother will like him, too.
- Simply put, you're feeling cautious.

- What about from the friend's point of view? You feel kind of nervous but unsure. You're happy to spend the time with your friend and be a support, but you know nothing about his brother. You want to be there for your friend, but the last thing you want to do is cause trouble or be a burden on his brother.

- One word: Supportive.

Step 3

Goal: Find a third position.

- Now imagine that you are an independent, neutral third-party observer outside of this situation, and see what you perceive.
- Notice how the behaviors of all parties interact and compare with one another.
- Notice the overall atmosphere, energy, and outcome.
- As before, describe it as simply as you can.

From the third position, you see that a simple miscommunication is unfolding. One brother assumed the meeting would be just the two of them. The other didn't, and brought along a friend for company, not realizing it would create awkwardness.

In one word: It's just a mismatch.

Step 4

Goal: Process.

- Now is the time to reflect.
- Go back to second position and look again at the facts, seeing if anything has changed.

- Then return to first position and see if anything has changed there. Is there any new information you possess? Do you have any new insights?

You can probably already see the value of this perspective switching.

If you had merely stayed in first position, you would have dwelt on the inconvenience you felt. By changing positions, you can appreciate that no hurt was intended, and imagine what things may look like from both your brother and his friend's point of view.

Can you see how this approach would lead you to behave completely differently from the way you might have otherwise?

Switching perceptual positions allows us to:

- Generate real empathy for people and situations.
- Figure out how to really connect with people.
- Understand the best way to communicate, or even resolve conflict.

If you can put aside your own perceptual position for a moment, you allow yourself the opportunity to *read* these actions rather than simply react to them from your own limited position.

One more amazing benefit? Perceptual position shifting is a powerful tool for analyzing people.

Depending on the rest of the context, you may uncover a whole world of information:

- You could learn about your brother's discomfort with intimacy.
- You could understand more about the friendship between him and his friend.
- You could even infer a thing or two about the friend and his level of conscientiousness or openness.

Gradually, you start to develop a working model of other people's personalities and positions, which are constantly interrelated. It's wonderful to think that, with the right mindset, conflicts and misunderstandings are actually nothing more than fascinating data points to feed into the big people-reading machine!

Chapter 4: Reading the Room (Group Dynamics)

We've already seen that behavior only has meaning *in context.*

➜ Something only means something when it's *relative* to something else.

That "something else" could be:

- The environment.
- The behavior of other people.
- The particular situation and circumstances.
- The perspective and worldview of the one engaging in that behavior.

In the Western world, we're trained to think on the individual level—to see people as discreet, self-sufficient units. While this perspective isn't "wrong," you're probably beginning to see that the intelligent people-reader uses an expanded view:

They see not just the individual, but the *network.*

Not just the figure, but the ground.

The entire system.

- Consider that words have definitions.
- That meaning is colored, shifted, and specified once we see it within a full sentence. The role it's playing and the context in which it exists is just as important as its technical definition.

It's exactly the same with human behavior.

- People have their own traits, characteristics, and "meaning."

- However, we can learn so much more about who they are when we "read" the rest of the sentence and paragraph—the way they're embedded in their social systems.

In this chapter, we're looking at how to read a person by reading the bigger social system that they're a part of. We'll do this by considering three main theoretical strands:

1. David Kantor's "Theory of Structural Dynamics"
2. Social dominance and how to read it in non-verbal "attentional flow"
3. The concept of "group flow"

David Kantor's Theory of Structural Dynamics

David Kantor is a systems psychologist who has researched and written extensively in the field of group behavior. His unique contribution is the theory of Structural Dynamics, which he says describes the fundamental structures that underlie all communication.

In particular, Kantor and his colleagues have identified four distinct "player roles" in any group situation. He termed these "action stances," explaining that the dynamics between these four types tells you not only about each player, but also about the way the group communicates, makes decisions, or overcomes conflict.

The four types are:

- **Mover**

- o The action here is to *initiate*, push the conversation forward, and create change and movement.
- o This is the person who starts things off, makes a plan, proposes an activity, or sets the agenda for the group.
- o These people are "directors." They can be helpful in organizing and motivating a group, but can also come across as bossy or impatient.

- **Follower**
- o The action here is to *support* the mover's initiation, validate it, and build on it.
- o While the mover kicks things off, it's the follower who follows through, and usually completes, that initiative.
- o These are the people who excel at collaboration and teamwork. The downside is their pliability, reticence, and, occasionally, passive aggression.

- **Opposer**
- o The action here is to *challenge* the move initiated by the mover and supported by the follower.
- o This is the "spanner in the works" who identifies flaws, suggests corrections, or asks pointed questions.
- o The downside is easy to imagine: opposers can get stuck in arguments and useless analysis, or become overly negative and critical.

- **Bystander**
  - The action here is to *observe* and *reflect*, providing a kind of meta-observation of the interaction itself.
  - These are the people who bring reflection, context, and the "bigger picture."
  - Though they provide a valuable objective perspective, these players can also be overly detached and aloof, even veering into being judgmental.

Chances are, simply reading these descriptions has you thinking about *your* role in certain groups, as well as the repeatable patterns you've witnessed in your family, work, or friend groups.

Kantor's theory is about changing the focus of observation. Instead of attending to the individual, you become curious about the nature of the relationships between individuals, i.e., the *links* on a network, rather than the *nodes*.

Kantor's theory is rather complicated, but for our purposes, we can boil it down to a few key principles:

- It's about **balance**. No player type is better or worse than another. Rather, a well-functioning group tends to need all types. However, the proportions may vary!
- It's about **flow**. We're not talking about personality types or fixed character traits, but *roles*. Nobody is stuck permanently in a role; they can switch. In fact, the way they switch—the flow—is valuable information.

- It's about noticing where things get "**stuck**." Instead of trying to identify problem individuals or topics, look for bottlenecks and dysfunctional dynamics.

Importantly, the "actions" in this model are *vocal* ones—they're mostly about what people say. It's not the *content* of what is said that matters, but the *function*.

For example:

- Mover: "Why don't we...?" "I suggest we..."
- Follower: "I agree." "Good idea, what date do you think will work?"
- Opposer: "OK, but the forecast is predicting rain for the weekend." "Yes, but..."
- Bystander: "Looks like a plan is coming together..." "Seems like there's some disagreement about the exact date."

Kantor's model shows us a picture of what group communication looks like—when it works well and when it doesn't. While his interest is in groups, we can use this model to inform the way we read individuals in those groups.

What's more, we can use our understanding of these different roles to actively shape and influence the groups we're in by changing the roles we ourselves play, and by altering the "actions" we take in those groups. This way, we give ourselves yet another avenue for testing our people-reading hypotheses.

The next time you're in a group, zoom out and watch the group flow *as a whole*.

See if you can clearly identify not individual people, but the flow of their actions:

- Notice the initiative being made.
- Notice how that initiative is received by both the follower and the opposer.
- Notice the interaction between the mover, follower, and opposer.
- Notice how the bystander's contribution is to summarize, reflect, or review.
- Finally, notice any repeating loops or patterns.

A well-functioning group tends to have a lively interplay of all player roles. The mover initiates, the follower supports, the opposer provides a little friction, then the mover and follower adjust, recalibrate, and try again, all while the bystander reflects and brings objective perspective.

What about when things get stuck?

Here are some possibilities:

- **The move-oppose-move-oppose pattern** – everything the mover initiates is shut down by the opposer.
  - The problem here is a lack of followers or bystanders to call out what's happening.
- **The navel-gazing pattern** – a never-ending loop between follower and bystander, where the bystander reflects and the followers supports—it's friendly and nice, but soon there's not much to reflect on or affirm!
  - The problem is the lack of a mover to drive things forward.
- **The yes-men pattern** – the mover initiates and a team of followers blindly support and

validate. They even support and validate their support and validation of the mover!

○   The problem is that without an opposer, the plan goes ahead, even when it shouldn't. The bystander may look on and issue a passive warning, but it may not be enough.

You get the idea.

The more you observe groups, the more you'll see the same recurring patterns and loops emerging.

➜   Has a group conversation fizzled, gone weird, or lost its way somehow? Look at the group dynamics and be curious about *why* that happened. Who was missing? What role was overrepresented?

➜   Likewise, notice when a group interaction feels really positive, productive, and enjoyable. What was the ratio of the different players? What dynamics played out?

Now the question is: How does Kantor's theory overlap with what we already know about the four personality types?

Recall that earlier we outlined the four (very) basic personality types according to Luis Amaral's 2018 research:

1.   Average
2.   Reserved
3.   Role model
4.   Self-centered

Now, there is no automatic link between the role a person plays in a group and their personality type.

That said, there are certainly *patterns* and *correlations*.

- According to the OCEAN or Big 5 model, **Average** types are more neurotic, extraverted, sociable, and assertive, but not especially open.
  - This personality type may show up most often as the *follower*.
- **Reserved** types are agreeable, conscientious, trusting, likeable, and reliable, and lower in neuroticism, extraversion, and openness.
  - This mix of traits lines up quite neatly with the role of *bystander*.
- **Role models** are extraverted, open, agreeable, confident, and conscientious, plus low on neuroticism.
  - Role models are natural leaders and will more easily play the *mover* role.
- **Self-centered** types have low agreeableness, low openness, and low conscientiousness, but may have high extraversion.
  - Being disinclined to agree and harmonize, this is the personality type most likely to play the *opposer* role.

If you observe somebody playing the bystander role in a group, does that automatically imply that they're a reserved personality type? Or if someone is repeatedly initiating, does that mean that they're a role model?

Of course not.

But it's a data point!

Later in Chapter 9, we're going to take a look at different behavioral programs, ingrained cognitive patterns, and fixed filters through which people may view their reality. By understanding these "meta-programs" we can start to see *why* someone may consistently play the same role in social groups.

By reading their behavioral choices in the social context, we can get a glimpse into the "perceptual software" they're running behind the scenes—i.e., how they make decisions, what motivates them, how they understand power and control, how they like to work, what they think of other people, and how they view risk and reward.

Watch Where Attention Flows

There's a persistent misconception out there, and it goes like this: The one who talks the most is the most important.

We automatically assume that the loudest, most talkative ones in a group are the most dominant, and the quietest ones are the least central or significant.

The truth?

It often has nothing to do with talking!

Instead, this chapter is all about paying attention to eye contact—where people are *looking*.

Someone may be talking a lot... but are people listening?

Someone else may be relatively quiet... but are all the talkers in the group subtly sparring for their approval?

Research on relational communication (Dovidio & Ellyson, 1982; Dovidio et. al., 1988) shows that dominance in groups is often signaled not by talk-time, but by "Visual Dominance Ratio" (VDR).

➜ **VDR** – The percentage of time spent looking at a partner while speaking, divided by the percentage of time looking while listening.

A person with high visual dominance tends to look at their partner more while speaking and look away more while listening, whereas a lower-status person often looks more while listening.

Essentially, VDR is a measure of power in social interactions. The higher the VDR, the higher the social status and dominance. The VDR is a way to visualize increased attention flowing towards higher-status individuals—in the form of people looking at them more intently when they speak.

The most influential person in the room isn't always the one talking; it's the one everyone *looks at* for approval after someone else makes a point.

It's the one everyone is hoping is listening when they themselves talk.

It's the one people consider influential, expert, or superordinate—and they show that by closely attending to every word they say.

➜ Pick a person in a group to watch, and look carefully at what happens when they speak.
➜ Notice if they are making firm and consistent eye contact with someone else as they speak.
➜ Notice where their eye contact goes when they are listening to others speak.

If the person *looks more while speaking than they do while listening*, they may be in a dominant position in the group.

If the person *looks more while listening than they do while speaking*, they may be in a more subordinate position in the group.

Essentially, you want to look for one tell-tale submissive behavior: close eye contact and attention on a speaker.

Those who are confident and dominant make much less of this eye contact when listening, and tend to look more directly into people's eyes when they're the ones who are speaking.

What matters is not the absolute time spent on either looking or not looking, but rather their *ratio*; you'll need to observe for a little while to get a sense of which a person does more than the other.

VDR is a metric that was initially studied under laboratory conditions. Being realistic, this may be difficult to recreate in ordinary life, where conversations are fleeting and there's often "a lot going on." Nevertheless, we can learn a lot about people and the groups they're in by noticing the "attention economy" i.e.:

- Where is most of the attention and awareness going?
- Which speaker tends to command everyone's attention the moment they open their mouths?
- Who is repeatedly looked at, even by people who are having conversations with others?

When you switch your lens from verbal to nonverbal communication, you will start to see these invisible patterns and flows—you will see who the room "votes" for with their eyes, and where the balance of attention really is.

Returning to Kantor's theory, any player can be the most dominant or high-status in a group—i.e. they can be movers, followers, opposers, or bystanders. However, the most likely pattern is that the mover takes center stage and leads, and the others pitch both their verbal and their nonverbal communication *in that direction.*

- Followers support and validate, and keep their eye gaze fixed on the mover and the initiative they're proposing.
- The opposer appears on the surface to be against the mover, but they nevertheless center the mover. In fact, the opposer would be lost without the mover to push against!
- The bystander might appear superficially to be independent, but their reflection inevitably centers around the mover's action. The bystander might share their observations with the group, but look at the mover to subtly seek their recognition and approval.

The mover, on other hand, if they are dominant in the group, will display a subtly different eye contact style: They will talk to each member of the group in turn with full eye contact, but, when being spoken to, they may look away while listening, almost as though their own eye contact is turned inwards, towards themselves. This is a very subtle gesture of recognition of their *own* dominance!

It's always a surprise the first time you see this nonverbal "inward gaze" behavior out in the wild, but once you learn to recognize it, you may start seeing it everywhere.

Now, as fascinating as all this is, what can we do with it?

- Want to understand the power dynamic between two people?
  - Watch their respective eye contact as they listen to each other speak. The one who looks away the most while listening will have the social upper hand in some way.
  - Look at the lines of attention. Imagine invisible arrows and look at where they're pointing. The most influential person in a conversation may not even be *in* that conversation!
- Want to increase your own perceived status?
  - Identify the mover and align yourself with their initiative or, if there isn't a mover, become one for the group. Make a suggestion, lead in some small way, or bring fresh energy into the interaction by sharing something bold or unexpected.
  - Avoid staring intently at people as you listen to them. Sparing and strategic eye contact will be more impactful, and will subtly convey that you are not subordinate.
- Want to resolve conflict, misunderstanding, or tension?
  - Consider that a dysfunctional group may be struggling with power plays or role confusion. Adopt a blend of the bystander and mover roles and gently make observations to shift stalemates. "There have been some really good

       suggestions so far, but why don't we shelve this issue for now and come back to it when we have more information?"

- o   Remember that if you're seeing a certain kind of imbalance or disruption in a group, you have the option to *step away*. You can become aware of where attention is flowing, you can direct your own attention as you see fit, and you can also *withdraw attention*.

Understanding "Group Flow"

A group is an organism.

It's composed of different "organs" that serve different functions, and it can act and move as an entity distinct from these components.

Lavoie and colleagues recently published an article in *Academy of Management Review* (2024) exploring the concept of "group flow."

Following on from Mihaly Csikszentmihalyi's popular theory on personal flow, group flow explores what this state looks like for collections of individuals working together.

According to Lavoie, a group in flow:

- Feels effortless, its movements swift and fluid.
- Reaches a peak of seamless collaboration.
- Has a momentum of its own—every contribution builds on the previous one.
- Performs effectively at a shared task.
- Shows a synchrony of contributions from each member.

- Creates positive emotions, i.e., feelings of being connected, motivated, and energized.

The opposite of flow is "group leakage", i.e. a state where interactions feel:

- Badly timed
- Uncoordinated
- Uneven
- Awkward
- Uncomfortable
- Unproductive
- Clumsy

Groups without flow are tense.

They're effortful.

They lack *consensus*.

The expression "the whole is greater than the sum of the parts" perfectly describes a well-functioning group in a flow state. The corollary also describes "group leakage"—a poorly coordinated whole is somehow *less* than all the parts that go into it.

Naturally, the concept of group flow is of interest to team managers and organizational psychologists. Their question would be, *how do we create and sustain group flow for maximum performance?*

But how can we use these insights when it comes to being skilled people-readers? How can we use an understanding of the group organism to help us better understand the individuals that make it up?

> ➜ **Core idea: Focus on moment-to-moment mini-interactions.**

Pay less attention to outcomes and more to what is unfolding in the present.

Lavoie et. al. explains how the magic of flow happens in tiny movements, which he calls "micro-dynamics."

Zoom in on these micro-dynamics:

- **Responsiveness:** Does each contribution show genuine engagement of and reaction to the previous one? Is there a real conversational back and forth, or are people just "monologuing together"? Good flow means people build on one another's contributions.
- **Timing:** Look at how the pieces of every conversation emerge relative to one another in time. Are people "synchronized dancing" or are they each free styling to their own song?
- **Unity:** Are people increasingly mirroring one another and matching their responses? Or is there friction, interruption, or an imbalance in contributions? A group flows when everyone's attentions and efforts are coordinated towards the *same goal*. Does the group share this single goal, or are there really several smaller, fractured groups?

What's fascinating about this way of looking at things is that it completely removes the personality element from the equation. It makes no difference if participants are introverted or extraverted, if they're thinkers or feelers, or if they're abstract or concrete.

What matters is how they flow together.

One of the ironies of learning to read people is actually learning to read energy flows, dynamics, and movements instead.

You'll know that a group isn't working when:

- People talk over and past one another.
- There are long, awkward silences or speech overlaps—or both.
- Certain ideas are raised only to get quickly dropped or ignored.

Why?

Because the contributions of each player are failing to connect with one another.

The flow is an energetic flow, and it goes beyond how dominant a person is, what they're saying, and how much they're saying it.

The mismatch is not between people, it's between people's *contributions.*

Having real social intelligence means looking way beyond personalities and egos—especially your own. It means understanding that there is more to a good conversation than just saying something interesting or intelligent. Instead, Lavoie's theory shows us that timing, harmony, balance, and flow are much more important.

Pay attention to the group flow and you'll always know when and how to speak.

We can't take responsibility for the character of the whole group, but we can play our part:

- Make contributions and comments that *link* to something that came before. Acknowledge and extend what others have shared to build momentum.
- Watch out for playing too much of the opposer role. Say "yes and" instead of "yes but."
- Notice when a contribution has been ignored, and deliberately pick it up and integrate it. Not only will you create more cohesion, you'll also be doing a favor for the person who made the contribution!
- Avoid interrupting, or talking much faster or slower than others. Pasue a moment before responding. Think of conversations as music— there should be a nice flowing interplay between sound and silence.
- Notice people's body language, tone of voice, language choice, and gestures, then mirror them. This will create feelings of emotional harmony.
- Practice real listening. Ask thoughtful follow-up questions that don't just reflect, but expand on what you've heard. Send the conversational tennis ball back over the net and give the other person something to play with!
- To avoid disruptions and disconnects, remind yourself to *add, not replace*. Too many people are in a hurry to one-up one another, or jump in with an anecdote they think is related, but really just switches attention back to them. Don't do this; instead of supporting your own ego, think of yourself as supporting the shared flow of the conversation. It's a team sport.
- Use body language that signals assent and cohesion. Nod, verbally affirm what you hear,

and say things like, "As you said..." to keep things feeling stitched together.

Understanding group dynamics helps you better place yourself within that group.

One way to practice this skill is to quietly (and politely!) observe groups from a distance, when you yourself are not included. This can be done in any public space, so long as you observe unobtrusively.

For five minutes, pretend you are an anthropologist and simply observe, looking for flow, friction, and power exchanges.

Look at the roles people are playing.

Look at how each person is contributing, and how those contributions themselves are connecting—or not.

Learn to see these things and you will learn to see people in a far richer, three-dimensional way. You may even learn something valuable about yourself.

Summary:

- If you can remove bias, expectation, assumption, ego, prejudice, interpretation, and judgment, the better you will be at reading people.
- Distortions and biases (what we think we see) can get in the way of understanding what we are actually seeing. These biases include:
  - perceptual selectivity,
  - attribution errors,
  - stereotyping,
  - the halo effect,

- projection,
- perceptual sets,
- implicit personality theories,
- expectations, and
- perceptual defenses.
- To improve your perceptual accuracy:
- Work hard to know yourself and then cultivate genuine empathy for others.
- Confirm your perceptions are true and compare them against others'.
- Be curious, open-minded, and non-judgmental.
- Ask open-ended questions.
- Delay forming an opinion about people.
- Perspective taking is the ability to imagine another person's psychological viewpoint—not their life through our eyes, but their life through their eyes. Some ways to cultivate this skill include trying to understand the perspectives of characters in film and literature. You can also practice switching perspectives to gain insight into conflicts or relationships and understand other people's roles.
- The perceptual positions framework is a basic method for understanding another person's viewpoint. There are three—first, second, and third—and switching between them allows you a richer and more dynamic insight into any situation.
- Personality categories can help us simplify human behavior. One notable theory is the Big Five, or the OCEAN model, which rates people on openness to experience, conscientiousness, extraversion, agreeableness, and neuroticism. Luis Amaral and colleagues have suggested

four personality types based on how the Big Five traits usually cluster: "average," "reserved," "self-centered," and "role model."

- There are four players in Kantor's Theory of Structural Dynamics: movers, followers, opposers, and bystanders. Identify these roles, notice where attention is going, locate where power and dominance reside, and observe how contributions are connecting and flowing in the group generally.

Section 2

Chapter 5: The Four Functions of Behavior

In the previous chapter, we set about trying to understand what people are like.

Are they open-minded or more uncurious?

Are they "neurotic" or more emotionally even?

Are they agreeable or totally uncooperative?

But what you might notice from this way of thinking is that it is not dynamic in any way—it's about what people *are*, not what they *do*.

Especially as outsiders looking in, **we can gain real insights into people's characters by observing their behavior, their choices, and the way they behave.**

After all, how do we know that someone is conscientious?

We look at their behavior.

Someone who merely *felt* they were conscientious in some vague internal way wouldn't quite make the grade!

In this chapter, we'll consider a model of human behavior that approaches things from a new direction.

It asks:

1. How are people behaving?
2. *Why* are they behaving that way
3. Why do they keep behaving that way?

This theoretical shift is about seeing personality as a **functional** quality—i.e., as something that we have because it's useful to us in some way.

Understand the function that certain behaviors serve for a person, and you understand who they are.

But before we leap into an explanation of the four functions, let's take a moment to understand exactly what we're trying to achieve.

Consider this:

> *You see a person at a party who is laughing and talking loudly with a big group of people, regaling them with stories. What does it mean?*
>
> *Well, we could say it's proof that the person is outgoing and gregarious, or that they enjoy people. We might get carried away telling ourselves a complicated story about why that person is this way, what it means, and so on...*

One problem: The story we're telling may be completely biased. That's because we don't really know what is going on in the head of the person we're observing.

How on earth could we measure their internal state at that moment?

We might say "they're extroverted," but the person might actually be acting this way because they're nervous in social situations, and the only way they can reduce that anxiety is to fiercely control the situation—i.e., by dominating socially. They're not extroverts at all; their coping mechanism just makes it look that way!

This explains why some theorists have argued for the use of a "functional behavioral analysis" (FBA) instead of merely telling stories about observed external behavior.

FBA is about formulating a theory that explains the functional relationship between a person's behavior and their environment.

- It's not about static, standalone personality traits.
- It's about how a person responds to stimuli in their environment.

One way to think about this is to imagine a trait like extraversion.

Can one stand alone, by themselves, and *be* extroverted?

No!

Extraversion is something you *do*, and it's a dynamic response to the environment—which in this case also includes other people.

In the previous model, we assumed that people behave the way they do because that's just the way they are. But with this model, people behave the way they do because something in the environment instigates and supports that action. In fact, every time their action is supported this way, it's reinforced—no personality required, just habit!

While personality assessments and profiles might be useful when you're working on your own personal development and self-awareness, it can be tricky when trying to apply to other people because we cannot see into their heads.

➜ What we can do, though, is observe the behavior and its environment.

Let's imagine that there are **four functions of behavior**—access, escape, attention, and sensory.

- **Access** – This includes mainly tangible things—items you can literally see and interact with via your five senses.
- **Attention** – This is an interaction, praise, or any kind of feedback or signal from others. This could be anything from a slight increase in awareness and attention from other people to a full-blown reaction from them, or even their subsequent actions and conversations.
- **Escape** – This is about removing an unpleasant item, event, or stimulus from the situation— especially one that has been previously punished and discouraged. An obvious

example is the behavior of pulling your hand away from a hot fire. A less obvious example is turning down invitations from people who make you feel bad in subtle ways.

- **Sensory** – This function has no connection to outside factors at all, but rather refers to internal rewards within the body itself. The pleasure of a hug, for example, or the satisfaction of having solved a difficult puzzle.

Furthermore, we can take note of:

1. The antecedent (what comes before the behavior).
2. The behavior (what the behavior is).
3. The consequence or outcome (what the new situation was after the behavior occurred).

Setting things out this way, we can see that behavior can be:

- Rewarded or punished
- Reinforced or discouraged.

Behavior always has an effect on the environment— after all, that's why we do it! But the environment in turn has a response to that behavior.

Understand all of this, and you gain a deeper, functional awareness not just of the person or the environment, but of their interactive relationship.

All behaviors follow the A-B-C shape (Antecedent, Behavior, Consequence), but they will each be maintained by different functions—or a combination of functions.

Returning to our example, we can imagine that someone might choose to behave in a gregarious and extroverted way because the behavior serves two broad functions:

- **Escape** – Taking charge of social situations allows them to escape the anxiety that comes from other people potentially asking intrusive questions, steering the conversation, or making a big deal out of noticing that they are quiet and putting them on the spot.
- **Attention** – When this person behaves in this way, people tend to respond in predictable and comfortable ways. The attention they give is a lot easier to deal with than the awkwardness of being asked, "Why are you so quiet?" all the time.

Is the above person extroverted?

Yes, in a way.

But using functional behavioral analysis allows you to understand the **why** and **how** of the behavior, not merely the **what**. Many standup comedians and famous entertainers surprise their fans when they claim to be deeply insecure, private, or introverted individuals. That's because, just as in this example, those fans were only looking at the behavior and not considering what this behavior meant and *why* it was being used.

Let's zoom out.

How can we use the insights from this kind of behavioral analysis to improve our people-reading skills?

The principles are as follows:

- Every action has a reason for happening, so ask yourself what the reward or positive outcome is to see why it's in that person's interest to keep behaving that way. This tells you a lot about them.
- Why do we behave in the way we do?
  o Because of how that behavior feels.
  o Because of the response we get from our environment.
  o Because it gets us something we want.
  o Because it helps us to get away from something we don't want.

Try to understand the *function* of the behavior you're looking at and you will instantly understand it better.

Personality theories can only go so far. Certain behaviors may be identical in two people who are nevertheless behaving that way for completely different reasons.

Conclusion: You should avoid reading people in a vacuum. Their behavior cannot be separated from the environment in which it occurs.

<u>*How to Read People Using the ABC Model*</u>

Step 1: Identify the behavior

- Take note of what you're looking at.
- Observe, but without telling any stories or making any assumptions about what you're

seeing—or else self-confirmation bias will creep in.

"He's extroverted." → That's already a story and a conclusion.

"He is talking more loudly and more often than anybody else. He is steering the conversation. He is positioning himself in the center of the group . . ." → That's observing behavior and paying attention to what's happening.

Step 2: Collect data to help you establish the antecedent and consequence of this behavior

Now, in our example, if you had never met the person before, you would have much less data to work with.

But if you knew them? You could gather plenty of data and combine it with what you know about their behavior at all parties or with other people in general.

- You might notice how people respond to the loud, excited talking and storytelling.
- You might notice that the more stressful the situation is, the more animated this person becomes.
- You might even notice that a few years ago, this person was quieter, and people responded to him differently back then.

Step 3: Infer the function of the behavior

Now what?

You put all this data together and make an educated guess about *why* this pattern exists.

You could even make a hypothesis and test it.

- One possible hypothesis: "He behaves in an outgoing and extroverted way so that he can cope with and control anxiety-provoking situations."
- Test it: You observe how he behaves in less stressful situations, or with smaller groups.
- Gather data and analyze: Combine all your guesses with other observations and come to a conclusion about how the behavior is functioning. Is it evidence for the hypothesis?

When we use the ABC model to help us read people, we're focusing on what comes before and after a behavior.

We focus on what a behavior *means*, and how it *functions*.

The ABC model is often used by counselors and psychologists to help people get a handle on their own maladaptive behaviors. By understanding what triggers and what sustains unwanted behaviors, they give themselves the chance to change things.

You can also use the model in a more open-ended way—**by observing any one of the three components, you can make guesses about the other components, as well as gain insight into the person making those choices.**

Here are a few more common and straightforward examples to show how you can begin using functional behavioral analysis yourself when observing and reading others.

Example 1:

A five-year-old is cheeky and frequently interrupts the adults' conversation.

- Antecedent: The adults are not paying her any attention.
- Behavior: She does something silly or butts into the conversation.
- Consequence: The adults laugh and smile and say things like, "She's such a little character, isn't she?"

Your hypothesis for the function of this behavior: **attention**. The five-year-old reliably wins praise and positive attention from the adults when behaving this way.

Example 2:

Joe is meant to be coming out with you for an early morning run, but instead he's at home in bed, snoozing.

- Antecedent: He stayed up late the night before. He's currently in a lovely warm bed.
- Behavior: He continues to stay in the lovely warm bed instead of waking up to go run outside in the cold.
- Consequence: His running mates are annoyed with him. But also, he gets to stay a few more hours in the lovely warm bed.

Your hypothesis for the function of the behavior: **sensory**. It's not rocket science. Joe is doing what he is doing because it feels good.

Example 3:

Nicky does come along with you on the run that day. In fact, she seems completely jazzed up and ready to go.

- Antecedent: Nicky has been having marriage difficulties with Joe, and the two can barely stand to be in the house together these days.
- Behavior: She started the running group herself and has worked hard to motivate everyone to the cause.
- Consequence: She is grinning from ear to ear after the run, and as soon as it's over, she starts talking about tomorrow's run.

Your hypothesis for the function of the behavior: **escape**. Nicky might want to literally escape her bad marriage, but the running may also serve as a way to escape feelings of frustration, helplessness, and anger, and to give her a sense of purpose when life feels difficult.

Consider: If you had only relied on static personality analysis for any of the above examples, you would not have grasped the full situation.

That's because it might be the case that:

- The five-year-old is *not* especially outgoing.
- Joe is *not* lazier than average.
- Nicky is *not* a particularly energetic or motivated person.

Rather, each of their actions is a direct result of their interaction with the environment—and not with their abstract personality or character.

If you've ever found it difficult to read people because they tend *not* to follow patterns, this could be why.

→ **All of us will act against our normal baseline or in ways we're not accustomed to if it serves our purposes in any particular moment.**

That's why we need to consider not just the person in front of us or their behavior, but how they and their behavior are embedded into the environment.

If we bump into Nicky five years later and she tells us she never kept up her running routine, we won't be too surprised to hear that she has also gotten divorced!

Even in cases where you don't know people well and cannot guess what came before or what will happen later, you can still get a handle on their behavior by asking what function it serves, right now.

Begin with an assumption: **People make sense.**

We could also put it like this: **People behave as they do because, in some way or another, it's working for them.**

Yes, even those behaviors that seem completely self-destructive or illogical!

Example: Imagine you have a colleague at work who constantly second-guesses you and checks your work. You do the "perceptual positions" exercise described in the previous chapter, but you're still having a hard time empathizing, and you're beginning to get annoyed.

- It's annoying, but start by deliberately assuming that in its own way, your colleague's behavior makes perfect sense to him, even if not to you.
- All you have to do next is figure out what is *triggering* that behavior and what is *maintaining* it.

Not only will this analysis give you some insight into what's going on, but it might also hint at a possible way out of the dynamic once and for all.

- **Antecedent** – You are your colleague's superior, so you're often given more challenging or complex jobs. You also know this colleague would like to advance in their role someday but is new at the company and finding it challenging to distinguish themselves.
- **Behavior** – They stick their nose into your tasks, offering their "help" and "advice" even when it isn't requested.
- **Consequence** – When the task is finished, you typically submit it and get the praise, satisfaction, or reward that comes with it. You also notice that the colleague tends to hover around when you're receiving feedback on these tasks, and once or twice has said, "We did a good job!"

Are you beginning to get a sense of the function of this behavior?

It may be a question of **attention**.

When behaving this way, your colleague gets to indirectly participate in feelings of having done good work on a job that he does not strictly have access to. This might satisfy a whole host of his needs, such as feeling relevant or convincing himself that he is learning and advancing, even if his actual job title doesn't reflect it.

Two things emerge from this analysis.

- First, you realize that this colleague must be feeling some sort of insecurity about his position and is perhaps frustrated in his work.
  - Is he struggling to get promoted?
  - Does he not feel recognized in his own tasks?
  - Is his work not challenging enough?
- Second, you start to see a solution to your problem (or a way to test your hypothesis).
  - You simply ask your boss to deliver feedback to you privately. If your theory is correct, the colleague will soon stop the behavior because there will no longer be the same consequence reinforcing it.

Let's say you do receive private feedback... and the behavior continues. Now what?

You throw away your hypothesis and make a new one.

Could there be a more internal sense of satisfaction that is driving this person (i.e., a sensory function)?

Could they perhaps be trying to impress you directly (attention function, but in a different way than you first thought)?

Either way, you are closer to understanding their real motivations than if you merely looked at the problem through the "personality type" lens.

Chapter 6: Learning to Read Emotions

Let's change gears once more and consider another rich and nuanced channel of data that we can mine whenever we observe our fellow humans: emotions.

Nonverbal communication and expression provide us with a world of information about a person.

What's more, emotion and behavior are linked.

Everything we do that's visible is behavior.

That includes things like:

- Facial expressions
- Gestures
- Tone of voice
- Body posture
- And everything else!

Learning to read body language is kind of like learning to read *the behavioral component of emotion.*

To put it another way: Our physical attitude in the world is an expression of our internal emotional state.

Now, this may seem like a very obvious point to labor. Is it really so earth-shattering to suggest that people's emotions influence their behavior?

Well, yes!

Especially when we consider how often we all ignore this kind of information in favor of listening to the words people say, or assuming that what they think and feel is the same as what we think and feel.

Never underestimate the power of bias and assumption to spoil the most obvious observations!

The best thing about reading body language is the way it reveals emotions:

- Spontaneously
- Unconsciously
- Unintentionally

That means you can trust it.

What if what you observe in someone's nonverbal expression differs from what they're communicating verbally?

➜ Well, you can read this mismatch itself as a point of interest.

Verbal/nonverbal mismatches can reveal:

- Deception
- Ambivalence
- Confusion

- A desire to conceal

Again, context matters; if someone sees something funny during a funeral but does their best to keep a straight face anyway, this is obviously not a question of deception but plain etiquette.

One way to think about body language and emotions is to imagine that human beings only ever express themselves on a single broad continuum, which you can understand loosely as **open or closed**.

- Open: Broad, loose, expansive gestures suggest:
  o Confidence
  o Excitement
  o Happiness
  o Relaxation
  o Trust
- Closed: Compacted, tight, tense, retreating, and cowering postures suggest:
  o Disgust
  o Fear
  o Shame
  o Sadness
  o Fatigue

Simply being aware of the patterns of relaxation and tenseness in people will clue you in to the more subtle emotions they may be feeling.

In fact, some theorists (Schutz, 1958) go so far as to suggest that persistent patterns of either psychological tension or relaxation actually settle and calcify in the body.

The person who is *constantly* angry, critical, or suspicious? They may end up with a literal line across their forehead or between their eyes.

The person who is *constantly* fearful and unconfident? Their slouching and cowering posture may almost become a permanent part of their comportment.

The person who is *constantly* smiling and laughing? Their smile lines reveal a lifelong habit of being expansive, happy, and receptive.

Think about that the next time you see someone who is chronically hunched, has an eternally tight neck and shoulder muscles, or a jaw that seems perpetually clenched.

However, let's now take a look at some common behaviors that are expressions not of people's overall behaviors or personalities, but of how they are feeling in that moment.

- Withdrawal, fidgeting, and plenty of small, unnecessary movements → **inhibition and anxiety**.
- Slow, sparing movements that lack energy and don't seem designed to reach out or connect in any way → **depression or exhaustion**.
- Fast, expensive, spontaneous, energetic movements and plenty of assertive, confident, and even affected (i.e., almost faked) gestures → **elation, joy, self-assuredness**.
- Fiddling with hair and skin, wrangling and twisting hands over themselves or holding them in tight fists, or plucking at clothing,

eyebrows or objects → **stress, repressed anger, or irritation.**

- A bent and collapsed body, a slight pout, angled shoulders, and a general vibe of slouching → **sadness, defeat, and worry.**
- Recoiling slightly, lifting the upper lip, wrinkling the nose, and raising the shoulders → **disgust or fear.**

Of course, all of this is relative and context dependent.

Wringing your hands and shaking your head at a ball game is totally different from at someone's death bead.

One clever trick for reading facial and body expressions: simply mimic the gesture yourself and see what emotion it invokes within you.

Try it right now. Gently touch the fingers of both hands to your lips, raise your eyebrows, and let your mouth open a little.

What emotion do you feel?

If you said "surprise" or even shock or horror, then congratulations, you may be more emotionally literate than you think!

Cultivating "Emotional Granularity"

Pretty much everyone knows that someone who is screaming and holding their hands to either side of their face is probably terrified. But to be masterful at people-reading, you **need to have a broad and deep knowledge of many different shades of emotion, as well as the ability to distinguish between them.**

The trick is that being able to read all the subtleties of emotion in other people requires we be fairly emotionally literate ourselves.

We can become aware of an emotion and describe it accurately:

- Sadness

Or, we can go much, much further, and identify it as:

- Despair
- Apathy
- Misery
- Resentment
- Sorrow
- Grief
- Disappointment
- Uneasiness
- Dismay
- Anguish
- Cynicism
- Gloom...

It's about learning to identify a richer palette of emotions. If we understand sadness as a primary color, for example, it's like learning to see all the infinite shades of that color that are possible, as well as how it may combine with other colors.

It's true that some people are simply better equipped to understand emotions, but that absolutely does not mean it's something that can't be learned. What's more, the real skill is not just possessing a big vocabulary; it comes in learning to interpret certain expressions and gestures *in context.*

For example, we saw above that someone behaving in an outgoing and extroverted way doesn't mean that this is simply their personality. Rather, in that example, it was a coping mechanism that served a particular function.

A smile doesn't always mean happiness.
Tears don't always mean sadness.
Frowning doesn't always mean anger.

But, noticing these things adds one more data point and, taken together with all your other observations, brings you one step closer to understanding people.

Here are a few ways to train your emotional granularity and expand your emotional vocabulary:

- **Exposure**. Read or listen to thought-proving content that uses specific terms to describe feelings. Keep track of your own responses to various stimuli, both verbal and nonverbal.
- **Fine-tune.** Become curious about the slight differences between similar emotion words. What's the difference between *content* and *satisfied*? Between *regret* and *remorse*? Pinpointing the difference heightens your emotional granularity. One surprising way to do this is to try new and unusual foods. Have

you ever noticed how rich the vocabulary is for describing wine? It's the same skill!

- **Build your vocab.** Research words in other languages that could apply to the way you feel right now. By learning new words, you can give your brain more options for predicting and perceiving emotions.
- **Become "sensitive."** Think of emotions as occurring on a continuum, and build awareness about where you are on that continuum. If one day you feel, say, bored, try to imagine what that feeling would be if you dialed it up one notch, then another. It might turn into "frustration" or even, at the very high end, something like "resentment." Can you discern the difference all along the scale?
- **Make friends with a thesaurus**. It seems strange, but looking at synonyms for emotions in a thesaurus can give a finer grasp on the subtle differences. Let's say you're talking to someone one day, and then pause to try to put a word to their emotion. You choose "pensive." You see that some synonyms include "thoughtful" and "contemplative." This is true, but you also sense a certain distraction in the person. You search around further and settle on different words like "distant" and "detached." Just by fleshing out the various possible adjectives, you're getting a deeper sense of a person's experience—while improving your vocabulary!
- **Use your imagination**. Finally, read fiction and watch movies. Pick a character and challenge yourself to describe how they feel in

five words. See if you can track that character's emotions as the story develops.

<u>*The Real Way to Read Body Language*</u>

Gestures are the body's "emotions."

It makes good sense to look at the body any time you want to understand what someone is feeling. However, most body language advice out there is very one-dimensional:

- A woman is playing with her hair? She must be flirting.
- Someone has their arms crossed? They're standoffish, stubborn, or maybe angry.
- A person looks up and to the left when talking? They might be lying.

But if we're using the "X always means Y" approach to reading body language, we won't get very far.

- The woman may be nervous and distracted.
- Someone may cross their arms because they're cold or trying to hide a stain on their shirt.
- A person may be looking up and to the left because they're embarrassed that you clearly think they're lying!

In other words, it's not that these observations are *wrong*, just that they only really "mean" anything when considered as part of a more complex whole.

→ **Key inisight: You are never merely reading an individual, but reading that individual's behavior and orientation within their environment.**

What does it mean to consider context?

If someone is sitting with their legs sprawled wide on the chair and their belly hanging out, it means two very different things if they behave that way alone in their own living rooms, or on a subway train crowded with people.

Looking at your watch when you're standing waiting for the bus means one thing, but a totally different thing when you do it seated at a restaurant with a date.

Frowning denotes one thing when you do it during a difficult exam, and another thing when you're listening to someone ask you a big favor.

→ Basically, what a thing ever "means" depends heavily on *who* is doing it, *when*, *how*, and *where*.

So let's think about expression and gesture as contextual. Here are a few questions to ask to help you gain more insight into the nonverbal expressions you observe in others.

Question 1: How does their expression compare to everyone else's?

In a group social setting, notice a person's expression relative to the consensus group expression.

- Is someone talking much louder or quieter than everyone else?
- Are they adopting a very different posture?
- Are they dressed in a very different manner?
- Are they speaking in a way that doesn't match or mirror those around them?

Pay attention to any discrepancies of this kind because they will tell you a lot about what is going on with that person.

Combine your observations with any insights about the function of their behavior.

> **Example:** If someone is being way more polite and deferential than everyone else and is smiling a lot more, this may signal an intention to win approval, escape criticism, keep the peace, or else slip beneath the radar.

You might confirm this hypothesis if you also see them constantly fretting to offer people drinks or using plenty of defensive and protective body language (for example, shrugging the shoulders as though to lower and hide the self while extending the hands outward, palms open, as though to say, "I come in peace!").

By making these observations, you're not only noticing how this person probably feels right now (nervous, vigilant, conciliatory) but also the role they play in this group or in life in general.

Example: Imagine you see a family out and about. Mom, Dad, and two of the children are smiling and laughing, and they have open, relaxed postures and expressions.

One child, though, is unsmiling and has tense muscles around their forehead and mouth. This discrepancy tells you that there is something on which this child disagrees with the rest of their family.

What is it?

Notice what else is going on and try to find the source of the difference. If the unsmiling child is the eldest teenager, dressed in goth clothing, you can begin to piece together a puzzle about the role this child is presently playing—not to mention the way the other family members are responding to it.

Question 2: How is their nonverbal expression a response to stimuli in the environment?

People seldom stand in an empty room and have an emotion.
The emotion is almost always *in response* to something.

The way people react to things in their environment tells you a lot about them. Again, it's not rocket science, and we can infer a lot simply by considering the degree of openness or closedness, tension or relaxation.

Example: What can you infer about a person who makes fists and tucks away their hands when someone teases them and puts them on the spot?

→ They are probably not enjoying the challenge/attention.

Example: What about when someone leans in to whisper something in another person's ear, and that person responds by leaning in even closer?

→ They are probably feeling (more than) happy with the escalation of intimacy the original gesture symbolized.

"People-watching" is a great way to fine-tune this skill:

- Simply pay attention to people walking, shopping, or eating in cafés.
- Pick someone and see how they respond to other people, to everyday tasks, and so on (politely and unobtrusively, of course!).
- Try to guess what they are feeling given the way they react to things around them.

You can do this in a smaller, more controlled way every time you converse with someone. Make a small change in the interaction, then watch closely to see how the other person responds to it.

A small change could be:

- Touch them lightly on the forearm
- Change the topic

- Ask a slightly more personal question

Make a small change and then watch for changes in *them*.

> **Example:** You tell a little joke in which you reveal some harmless but embarrassing detail about yourself, but you notice that the other person remains stoically unchanging in their expression (i.e., they don't laugh, act shocked, or share a similar story of their own). How do you interpret this?

> → You might guess that they are not interested in the slight escalation of intimacy this move suggests.

When you later lean back, adopt a more formal tone, and lessen eye contact, you note they become more relaxed and even start smiling.

> → More evidence for your hypothesis! They're clearly happy with the status quo.

Question 3: How is their nonverbal expression unusual or mismatched?

Often, the most noteworthy aspects of a person's experience are those that are

- Unusual
- Heightened
- Somehow unexpected

Pay attention if someone's responses to something seem (to you, anyway) mismatched.

Are they very relaxed in a stressful situation?

Smiling whilst getting reprimanded?

Enormously offended by a compliment?

Look closer and see what you can infer from this apparent discrepancy.

People will often respond in exaggerated ways when the matter somehow concerns:

- Shame
- Confusion
- Anger
- Fear

Defensiveness in general strongly suggests a lack of confidence or feelings of vulnerability. On the other hand, people who seem to show *too little* emotion may be telling you something important about how they're coping.

> **Example:** Imagine that you notice that someone is getting extremely flustered and stressed while trying to save a phone number on their mobile phone. You notice the irritability and clumsiness, and how they then almost give up when their first attempt doesn't work. They're blushing, almost angry.

You factor in your other observations:

- they are an older person,
- they're unfashionably dressed,
- they're retired, and
- the mobile phone is very old and damaged.

You conclude that this total overreaction to the annoyances of technology may say something about this person's discomfort and resentment of modern life.

Perhaps they are embarrassed by their lack of ability, or perhaps you can infer that they have never bothered with certain material trappings because they prioritize other values.

Perhaps their reaction tells you something about their attitude toward *you*—do they worry that you will think they're just a foolish old person who will get annoyed and impatient with them?

Whatever it is, this little detail about the phone is a clue, and can help you build a rich and nuanced picture of the person in front of you.

- Stay alert to overreactions.
- Watch out for underreactions.
- Pay attention to reactions that are just odd, unusual, or unexpected.

Example: You're with someone when you both experience something sudden and frightening, like an attempted mugging or an earthquake. You notice that not only is the other person *not* frightened, but they seem to actually be enjoying it!

What could this tell you?

Possible hypotheses:

- This person is a thrill seeker
- They have a high tolerance for risk, danger, and novelty
- They're maybe even a little bored or depressed in life, and their lack of response to danger points to a kind of apathy or emotional numbness

On the other hand, if the person leaves the situation completely distraught, talking nonstop about what *they* experienced and how traumatized *they* are, you can guess they are pretty self-focused or like to imagine themselves as victims!

Why You Can't Always Trust Facial Expressions

Way back in 1972, with the publication of *The Expressions of the Emotions in Man and Animals*, Darwin first suggested that human emotions map onto distinct facial expressions. The trouble with humans, though, is that we may be in situations where we wish to conceal our emotions, or else appear to be feeling ones we aren't.

Richard Restak, the author of *Mozart's Brain and the Fighter Pilot: Unleashing Your Brain's Potential*, provides a simple exercise designed to improve your ability to read other people's emotions. Restak claims that,

"When a person pretends an emotion, he or she activates the same brain areas that would be activated in circumstances when the emotions are naturally and spontaneously expressed."

Try this exercise.

- Get a trusted friend and position yourself around three feet away from one another.
- Have your friend close their eyes.
- Look at your friend's face and ask them to think about the saddest memory they have of their life, but also instruct them that they shouldn't respond in any way—for example, by sighing or frowning.
- Watch their face and see if you notice any subtle changes.

Make a note of what you observe.

- Next, ask your friend to completely clear their mind and think of nothing. Again, watch and see what you can see.
- Now ask your friend to open their eyes and look at you, again thinking about the saddest moment in their life, followed by a completely neutral experience, say, buying milk at the store.
- Finally, ask the friend to imagine the happiest moment of their lives. Throughout, keep a close watch on their face, especially the eyes. In particular, notice what happens in the moments when one emotion *shifts* to another.

The exercise is also illuminating when you switch roles.

What did you both notice?

Is there anything you're especially surprised by?

You may find that what your friend tells you they were thinking about and what you perceived in their facial expression were *totally at odds.*

For example, from your perspective, they might have seemed totally serene and confident, but they tell you they were at that moment recalling the distressing moment they learned their grandmother had died.

You'll notice this the other way around, too, and be surprised at how poorly your friend read your expressions. Sure, in hindsight you may be able to read certain subtleties in an entirely different way. But what if you were *only* relying on your reading of their facial expression?

The point of this exercise is not to show you that facial expressions are meaningless and that it's not worth paying attention to them. Rather, **it's to show just how hidden people's true emotions can actually be.**

The exercise shows you how well people can conceal their actual emotions, even when you think you may be seeing something in the movement of an eyebrow or the twitch of a lip.

Something else you might notice is that the transitions themselves provide more information than any single facial movement or gesture. In other words, what you might be discerning is the *effort* someone is making to conceal their emotions, or else the change from one emotion to another.

Even if someone is doing their best to hide their true feelings, you can still infer something when a stimulus gets some kind of rise out of them.

What does it mean?

Well, the rest of the context and all your other observations will help you find the answer.

> **Example:** You're having a disagreement with a family member because you strongly suspect them of lying to you. Let's say you're having a discussion, and their facial features are lively and animated.
> Then you bring up the issue of the lie, and this suddenly changes. Their face goes blank. They start making simple, clear, concise statements and repeating themselves.

What does their facial expression tell you? Well, nothing.

But the *sudden change from expressive to non-expressive* tells a big story. Even though the topic is distressing and you're unhappy, they don't mirror this or respond in a normal way to it.

What you are noticing is the lack of expression or, more accurately, the effort being made to create that impression.

What does it mean?

There is an attempt to minimize or hide something, or else to de-escalate the situation. This person may not be outright lying to you, but they are definitely trying to avoid showing you *something*.

We will explore this issue of lie detection in a later chapter, but first, we need to consider a very important concept in the art of people-reading.

Chapter 7: Baselining

Picture this. You meet someone new for the first time, and these are some things you notice:

- They are grinning ear to ear.
- They immediately start gushing about how much they love your shoes.
- When you start talking, they listen with rapt attention.
- They laugh (loudly) at all of your jokes.
- They tell you afterward that they have never met anyone quite so interesting as you.
- When you part ways, they make a big deal about getting your contact details and invite you to their house, but not before giving you an enormous hug to say goodbye.

Now, what do you think about such a person?

You probably assume that they really, really like you!

They seem ultra-friendly and positive and like they really enjoyed your company, or even that they're coming onto you. That is, until you meet this person again, this time in a group.

You see that they treat *everyone* this way.

Oops.

You suddenly realize that they don't think you're especially great—that's just what they're like with *everyone*!

But your interpretation wasn't exactly wrong. That behavior usually does indicate someone who is interested, positive, friendly, etc. But these in-a-vacuum observations don't tell you how common this behavior is *compared to that person's own tendencies.*
Perhaps, after watching them interact with other people for a while, you realize that they are a little *less* warm and friendly to you than they normally are in general. Your original reading was not just inaccurate, it was flat-out wrong.

It's important to consider any single behavior not just as it compares to other people or to the environment itself, but to the person behaving that way.

In other words, is this behavior common or uncommon *for them*?

We can't make any conclusions about the information we gather if we don't have something to compare it to. What seems normal to you might not be normal to them, and so on.

A baseline = A set of nonverbal behaviors (like posture, movement, and gestures) that a person usually uses when they are comfortable and relaxed.

It's like a person's default setting.

When you read body language, you are looking at expression in both absolute and relative terms. You decide whether something is noteworthy according to how far from the baseline it is.

If you observe the person above being polite and kind to someone, but with much less enthusiasm than they normally do, you can probably conclude that they don't like that person—even if their behavior is objectively friendlier than the average.

Body language experts agree that you should pay attention to the subtleties and *changes* in a person's body language to know when it's been activated or triggered during a normal conversation.

Notice all the ways in which they are behaving differently from what's normal for them.

➜ **Core idea: The clue lies in the deviation from baseline.**

The first step, then, is to establish a baseline wherever possible. Here are things to look for:

- Blink rate
- Eye contact—frequency and duration
- Breathing—both rate and depth

- Body movement speed and fluidity
- Facial expressions
- Gestures
- Cadence, pitch, volume, articulation, and rhythm of voice
- Overall posture—open or closed, tense or relaxed

Note, of course, that all of the above need to be considered *in context.*

So, someone's baseline when they are at work doing their teaching job may be completely different from their baseline on the weekend when they're with friends and doing a hobby.

It's difficult to establish a baseline for someone the first time you meet—you will typically need to spend more time with them in different contexts to begin noticing stable patterns.

That said, you can still use the principle of baselining even if you only engage with a person for a short time. For example, over the course of a twenty-minute conversation, you might establish a baseline *for that conversation,* and this allows you to detect when something suddenly changes.

- How does the end of the conversation compare to the beginning?
- How does their demeanor change when talking about different topics?
- How do they react to different members of the group?

Being aware of how people change over the course of a single interaction is also what will allow you to gracefully end the conversation at the right time.

<u>*Using Baselines to Detect Deception*</u>

The baseline approach is especially useful for one type of people-reading: catching liars.

Many people believe all sorts of myths about how you can catch a liar red-handed (they look up and to the left, they bite their lip, etc.), but these will seldom help you.

A better way to find out if someone is lying is to identify "leakage."

Leakage is *unintentional* and *inconsistent* communication across multiple channels like:

- facial expressions,
- gestures and body language,
- voice,
- communication style, or
- verbal statements.

A leak can be anything—but it is always something different from the baseline, something that was intended to be concealed but wasn't. Spot it, and you can infer a bigger concealment that may be underway.

Let's take a look at how this may play out in real life.

Step 1: Gather information

Everyone has a "norm": A basic, preferred setting for how they act when they are under normal amounts of stress.

This can be anything from how quickly they speak, to the words they usually use. What's more, a person often has a "tic," or a sign that they are uncomfortable, and too far from their "norm."

Have you noticed these tics or tells in your own family and friends?

- A quick smirk or frown when you say something they don't agree with.
- A tendency to suddenly muddle words when stressed.
- A certain kind of exaggerated smile that only appears when they're trying to control a situation.

But even if you see a tic, tell, or some other clue, keep looking. A tic doesn't automatically mean a lie. But it does tell you something—and what you continue to observe will help clarify what that something is.

Try to answer these questions:

- What is normal for this person?
- How does this change when they are experiencing stress?
- When and where do you see the most dramatic differences?

You may gather this information all at once in a single conversation, or you may need to get to know a person well first.

Step 2: Establish rapport

Now, if you were an FBI agent trying to uncover deception, you might need to quickly establish rapport to build on. Since you're probably not an FBI agent, just apply this step in whatever way suits your situation.

It goes without saying that if you have just met someone or don't know them well, your chances of finding out the truth will be greater if you can establish some kind of *shared understanding* and *connection* with them first.

This does two things:

- It puts you at ease → This allows you to be more focused and observant.
- It puts them at ease → This allows you to more easily observe their baseline.

Even if you already have an established relationship with the person, the way that you talk to them will make a big difference in how they communicate with you. Of course, at no point should you give any hint that you are trying to uncover deception.

- Be relaxed.
- Make eye contact, but not too much.
- Be warm and steady.

- Once the tone is set, gradually invite them to tell their stories.
- As they speak, listen with relaxed and respectful empathy.

If you are unguarded, they will be, too.

Ask open-ended questions rather than immediately grilling them about what you want to know. Don't come across as too forceful or determined.

One good way to subtly promote rapport is to mirror them in small ways—adopt the same posture, tone of voice, expression, or even verbal idiosyncrasies to show that you're on the same wavelength.

Step 3: Run through the baseline checklist

The following five-part checklist is about making as thorough an observation as possible, in as short a time as you can.

While you're making your observations, though, remind yourself that what you *don't* observe can be just as important as what you do! The general rule is to start your way at the top of the person and work your way down.

1. First, observe their **face:**

- What is the position of their head and how are they holding it?
- Are they touching their face? How and where? How often?

- Watch the eyes—where are they looking? How fast are they blinking?
- Do you notice any tension or looseness in the mouth?

2. Next, listen to their **voice:**

- What is the tone or character of their voice? Smooth, jerky, wavering, clear, monotone?
- Is the pitch low, medium, or high?
- Listen for both kinds of volume—loud or soft, but also how much talking they're doing.
- How fast or slow are they talking? Is their pace consistent or all over the place?

3. Listen to the **words** they're saying:

- Do they use verbal fillers (um, ah, like)? How often?
- Are they being formal or causal? Swearing?
- Do they use full sentences? Are the sentences unusually long or short?
- How is their grammar? For example, do they frame things in passive voice or state everything as a question?
- Do they use a lot of "I" and "me"?

4. Notice how they're holding their **body:**

- How much space are they taking up? Are they spreading out or collapsing? Rigid or yielding?
- Is their posture generally open or more closed? Tight or loose?
- Do they seem to be advancing or retreating?

- Notice their gestures—are they wide and expansive, or small, nervous, and useless?

5. Finally, take note of the **fidget factor:**

- Are there lots of unnecessary and pointless gestures? What kind?
- What do they do in a relaxed position?
- Is their overall impression one of movement or stillness? Relaxation or agitation?

Okay, great. Now that you've gathered all this data, what do you do with it?

➡ Your main goal as a deception detector is to *look for stress signals* that alert you to an inner state of effort, anxiety, or dissonance.

What does this mean?

Well, think about what it's like to lie.

If your brain is a computer, then lying represents an additional computational burden that asks your brain to work far harder than it would have to if it was just recounting the truth. In the same way that a CPU that is hard at work will sometimes make loud noises or start to get hot, you can learn to look for the human "stress signals" that tell you that some additional work is underway—potentially a lie.

Right away, you can see the first problem with using this approach—i.e., someone may be burdened with extra thinking not because they're lying but because they're unhappy for another reason, or simply nervous (perhaps because they sense you're interrogating them!).

Again, the only way out of this dilemma is to continually *observe the whole* and consider what you're observing, even making allowances for the fact that someone might be nervous for some other reason.

You always want to take into account:

- Social norms
- The impact of the context and environment
- The social role that person is currently playing
- What they may be trying to achieve with their behavior in general
- The nature of your relationship
- Their normal personal baseline
- Any other potential sources of stress
- The unique way their expression changes in response to stress

Once you've gathered information and established a baseline, your next move is to *watch very closely for anything that does not fit that baseline.*

The logic is that if you are familiar with how a person behaves when relaxed, then you can clearly notice when they are stressed and outside that range.

➜ **Key insight: Instead of jumping in with accusations, threats, and leading questions, try establishing a connection.**

You don't want to do anything to make them clam up. That's because if they then start behaving in a stressed way, you won't know if this is because they're genuinely lying, or just because it's stressful to be accused of lying!

Once you have established rapport and observed them in their relaxed and calm state, you'll be able to recognize changes in their behavior when you pose meaningful questions later. Though you don't need to practice this skill in the way that professional interrogators do, the principles are still the same.

> **Example:** Let's say you are interviewing a candidate for a role in your company, but you have reason to believe they're not being especially truthful on their resume. Now, you're not too concerned about the white lie—it's rather small—but you *are* concerned about the overall trustworthiness of the candidate and, bluntly, want to see how good they are at hiding the truth!

Either way, you will learn something interesting about them.

You begin with two simple questions:

- What's normal for this person?
- How do they behave when they're stressed out?

You prepare for the interview by reading up on them as much as you can beforehand, and try to make inferences based on their age, where they grew up, education, social media use, background, etc.

This can only take you so far, though.

You look at the way they've compiled their resume:

- You see what they are emphasizing (their degree and awards).
- You see what is de-emphasized or not mentioned at all (a gap of two years, their exact job title at a previous position, etc.).

➔ This tells you a lot about how this person wants to present themselves. What *aren't* they showing, and why?

You're making loose hypotheses, but no big conclusions yet. In the interview, you simply begin by getting to know them.

You keep things very warm and relaxed and even make out that you're not a seasoned interviewer and don't intend to take the process all that seriously.

You do what you can to put them at ease—smiling, eye contact, offering to make them a coffee, leaning in close, and making friendly small talk about relatable things...

But all the while this is happening, you are *watching*. You are paying attention to those five areas of observation to establish the baseline.

Now, you already know that an interview is a naturally stressful situation, so all you are doing is *looking for what the baseline level of stress is* before the "real interview" begins.

You notice:

- Lots of eye contact and smiling
- Leaning forward in the chair
- Voice medium loud, strong, even
- Fidgety hands
- Lots of "I" statements
- Lots of nodding along
- Tight but active overall posture; impression of alertness and energy

Great.

Conclusion? This is what the candidate looks like under the normal conditions of interview stress.

Once you're sure that rapport has been established and you have a baseline (i.e., run through the five-point checklist in your head), then you can start pressing on what you believe to be the deception.

You first ask about something that you know is true, and observe the response.

"So you went to Harvard."
"Yeah, I did."
"This was in... 2019? Okay, so I also see you took an extra year to complete your degree."
"Yeah, that's right. I was in quite a bad car crash and so I graduated a little later."

"I'm sorry to hear that. But it says here that you went straight from that into your position with the first startup, is that right?"
"Yeah, that's correct. Spring of 2020, I began work with *Real Time*."

While on the surface all this seems pretty run-of-the-mill, you are actually hard at work noticing the way the candidate responds to questions when it's the truth:

- Short, to-the-point answers.
- Frequently beginning with "yeah" and an energetic nod.
- Good eye contact.
- Alert posture.

This is important. It's what the truth looks like for this person, in this context.

Let's move on.

You say: "Well, we've been looking for developers like you for ages, so it would be great to have you on board. But I'm curious, it seems like your last role would have been more your speed, salary-wise at least. Why the change?"

Now, you play it cool.

You watch.

You notice these things:

- The candidate keeps smiling and making eye contact, but all at once, they lean back in the chair and fold their hands firmly in their lap.
- Their voice drops in volume and pitch.
- Their posture seems to spread and loosen a little.

Here's the candidate's response:

"There are a lot of reasons for that, the primary one being issues with their initial stages of funding. The company was bought out, but there was a lack of overall interest from investors. Long story short, I'm looking for a little more security regarding pay."

What to make of this answer?

Let's say that you happen to *know* that this is a white lie.

You know the founders of *Real Time* and know that although financing was tight at first, this particular employee was fired for completely unrelated reasons. It's not a big deal, but you make a note of this.

This too is important. It's what this person looks like when they're lying—or at least bending the truth!

Let's move on again.

You ask them some more questions, keep them at ease, and then you finally ask the question you are most interested in:

"If we offered you this role, do you see yourself remaining on for the foreseeable future? At this stage, we are really looking ahead at the long term, and we want to start bringing in people who can grow with us. Does that align with what you're after?"

Let's say the candidate does this:

- They lean back even further.
- They give another formal, long-winded answer, some of it in passive voice and delivered in a kind of low-energy way compared to their previous answers.
- They assure you they are very committed to the role.

You ask some further questions, and their demeanor changes again, back to what you have already registered as the "truthful," relaxed baseline.

So, does this mean they were lying about wanting to stay in the role for the long term?

It's not *conclusive...* but the evidence strongly suggests it!

Crucially, if you had simply followed ordinary body language (i.e., fidgeting and nervous, tight posture equals lying), then you would have gotten this completely wrong.

You would have assumed that the calm, relaxed-looking person who was speaking clearly and articulately was telling the truth. But for this person, whose natural state was more energetic and excitable, this relaxed body language was, ironically, a "stress signal" hinting at deception.

As you can imagine, learning to spot liars is more like a dark art that requires years of practice to master. At first, try not to think of it as "catching a liar." Think of it as becoming aware of people's patterns and shifting energies in any interaction or conversation.

Become good at noticing *changes* and *shifts*.

Learn to see the switch from normal to unusual.

Yes, this will help you become better at spotting lies, but it will more generally help you become a brilliant people-reader.

Chapter 8: Watch Wardrobe, Walk, and Food

"The clothes maketh the man," says the old proverb.

But that's not all that maketh him!

The way he walks…

The shoes he wears…

The food he eats…

The *way* he eats that food…

There are many additional cues and signs we can learn to read if we only pay attention. However, all the same rules about perception and non-verbal expression apply, and the goal is again to learn to observe people with genuinely fresh eyes.

<u>*Clothing Speaks*</u>

Jennifer Baumgartner, a clinical psychologist and author, has always been interested in the "psychology of dress." In her fascinating book, *You*

Are What You Wear: What Your Clothes Say About You, she explores this complex relationship:

- How psychology affects our clothing choices.
- How our clothing choices in turn impact our psychology.

In other words, it's a reciprocal relationship.

On a personal level, understanding how you are portraying yourself aesthetically is, she claims, as important as understanding your biases, beliefs, and communication style—in fact, clothing *is* a communication style!

Northwestern University explored the concept they called "enclothed cognition" in a recent study. In their report, researchers define it as *"the systematic effect that clothes have on the psychological processes of the wearer."*

Enclothed cognition = what your clothes say to you, not about you, and how you feel about them.

But for our purposes as budding people-readers, we can see that clothing is also a brilliant window into a person's current state of mind.

Let's imagine that we are extending our understanding of body language (gesture, voice, posture, facial expression) to include the choices a person makes every time they get dressed in the morning—let's call it fine-tuning our "enclothed perception."

Both Baumgartner and the researchers at Northwestern University make an interesting suggestion: You don't dress based on how you feel, but based on how you *want* to feel.

- Want to feel strong? Out comes the power suit.
- Sexy? Red dress, naturally.
- In control? Your best shoes, a grown-up watch, a knock-out scent.
- Relaxed? Your decades-old sweatpants and fuzzy slippers.

So far, so good. However, we are also interested in the fact that people do tend to pick clothing that mirrors their emotional state.

➜ Clothing is a reflection of an emotion, desire, belief, or intention.

As you can guess, there are some caveats (and they're not that different from the caveats we keep in mind when reading body language in general).

- Context matters—if people have to wear something as a part of their job or social role, it implies much less about them.
- Age, gender, ethnicity, social class, and background all play a role too—what is considered daring for one group may be conservative for another. What is expensive looking in one country may be casual in another.
- Historical period—obviously, our shared cultural understanding of what the vocabulary of fashion means will change over time!

Baumgartner also explains how it's not just the clothing itself, but the *way* a person wears that clothing. The messages are quite obvious when you stop to pay close attention to them.

Here are some examples:

- A person who never throws anything away, or is still wearing things from decades prior?
  - They may be clinging to the past in other ways, too.
- A person who only wears neutrals, "basics," and no accessories?
  - They may be stuck in a rut, or overly comfortable and complacent.
  - They may be overwhelmed and playing it safe to cope.
- A person wearing clothing that's too big for them?
  - They may have recently lost weight and are still adjusting.
  - They may have low self-esteem and a desire to hide themselves.
- Someone who consistently dresses to emphasize sex appeal?
  - They likely crave attention from the opposite sex.
  - They may see their own identity in these terms.
  - They may be insecure in this area and are trying to encourage others to see them this way.
  - Occasionally, this style can suggest that a person is playing out a role they feel they've been assigned in life.

- Dressing too "young" or too "old"?
  - This may hint at the age this person feels they are, or the age they wish to be seen as.
  - May point to signals around maturity, sex appeal, professionalism, or class.
- A person who basically only wears work clothes?
  - Their "uniform" tells you the role they are most commonly inhabiting. For better or worse, work is a big part of their identity.
- A person who is always wearing designer logos or expensive status markers?
  - They want you to treat them well.
  - They want to be seen as winners, or as though they belong to a special category above others.
  - They may be very goal driven and seek external validation and approval, basing their aspirations on conventional symbols of wealth and prestige.
- A person forever in jeans/tights and a relaxed hoodie or sweatshirt?
  - Unless they are literally coming back from the gym or a walk, assume this person has put their own vanity on the back burner and is focusing on something else, such as parenthood.
  - It *may* signal low self-worth, exhaustion, or a lack of purpose.
- A person deliberately wearing a symbol that connects them to a certain group?
  - Whether it's a band T-shirt, a religious necklace, a hat with a political slogan, or a tattoo of a meme—this person sees themselves as one of the group, but they are also signaling a wish for others to recognize that fact.

You get the idea.

Just as we do with every other behavioral observation, we need to interpret clothing *in context.*
  Example: You meet a woman wearing a torn blouse with shoulder pads, a tulle skirt, high top sneakers, and a crocheted handbag made of seashells. Her hair is full of untidy clips and bows, and she's wearing bright-red lipstick and horn-rimmed glasses.

Now, if the woman were 80 years old and wearing all this to her granddaughter's graduation, we might think that her choices signaled a kind of nostalgia, lack of connection to current trends, or else an endearing disregard for other people's opinions.

But if the woman were 23 years old and wearing this to a job interview, we would conclude something entirely different. We might wonder why she was so eager to communicate that she was different from the norm.

Is she a very dramatic person?
Insecure?
Flamboyant?
Genuinely unconventional and artistic?
A bit self-absorbed?

Your other observations will help you decide.

As with other body language, watch for changes from the baseline, or clothing that is:

- Out of sync with others, the occasion, the weather, or the culture
  o Someone wearing sexy pink heels to a midwinter funeral in a muddy field? That choice *means* something.
- Unexpected
  o A four-year-old wearing a top hat? There's definitely a reason.
- Exaggerated in some way
  o Your middle-class neighbor suddenly sporting a Patek Phillipe watch worth two million dollars? That's certainly a message!

Remember that *deviations from baseline* reveal the most information!

Example: You've gone on several dates with a person, and every time they've shown up super well-dressed and impeccably groomed. On the seventh date, they arrive wearing tracksuit bottoms and an old gym shirt.

They may suddenly be feeling more comfortable around you, or else they have unofficially abandoned "the chase" and decided that, for whatever reason, it was no longer necessary to impress you. It's not the clothing that speaks; it's the *shift* that matters.

And it's not just clothing.

A 2012 study investigated how well people are able to make character judgments about others just by looking at the shoes they wear most of the time. They concluded that a snapshot of a person's favorite footwear *can* reveal a lot about them, including their age, income, and even attachment anxiety.

On their own, shoes reveal a tiny amount of information about the wearer, but this information can naturally be quite useful when combined with other data.

According to Gillath et al., shoes are a pretty accurate thing to look at for good first impressions. Consider:

- **Flat shoes** indicate a humble person who gets things done without requiring supervision or praise.

- **High heels** can signal confidence, deliberation, ambition, and perhaps a need for attention.

- **Flashy shoes** can, naturally, hint that a person is an extrovert and likes to stand out.

- **Flip flops** point to a relaxed, easygoing attitude that may tend to laziness.

- **Shoes that are always squeaky-clean and polished** suggest the desire to make a good first impression and someone who takes care of their life and themselves.

- **High-heeled black ankle boots or "Chelsea" boots** may suggest confidence or even aggression. Often worn by people who know *exactly* what they want in life. On the other hand, tan or brown cowboy-style ankle boots are typically worn by more relaxed, artsy types.

- **Shoes that are in poor repair or constantly dirty** may suggest this person doesn't take care of themselves, either.

- **Formal lace-ups or expensive loafers**, especially if not in a professional context, are somber-looking "classic" shoes that suggest someone wants to be taken seriously and that they value tact, discipline, and order.

- **Sports shoes** could symbolize being goal-oriented and active, but if they're more like ordinary sneakers or street shoes, the person may be versatile and energetic and find it easy to get along with everyone. On the other hand, if those sneakers cost two hundred dollars, then the story they tell is a little different...

- **"Sensible" footwear** suggests that people are secure in themselves and internally motivated. Birkenstocks, for example, suggest someone loves comfort, the outdoors, and quality things—and that they prioritize comfort over style.

- **Barefoot**—well! Depending on the context, you could be dealing with a rugged outdoor type, a dedicated rebel, or a toddler...

Naturally, shoe choices will take on different meanings depending on time and place. In some parts of the world, at some points in history, red shoes were associated with prostitutes. Of course, if you saw red shoes on the pope (a centuries-old papal fashion), you would not make that association!

That's why observing shoe type is not enough on its own. We need to constantly keep an eye on the bigger picture.

Notice how people take care of their shoes—or not.

- Do they insist on wearing light-colored or delicate shoes that require constant cleaning? → See if you can notice signs of perfectionism, competitiveness, or obsessiveness in the rest of their behavior.
- Do they regularly toss their shoes to the side when they take them off, allow them to get dirty and broken, walk freely through dirt and water, or insist on wearing shoes that are ugly, inappropriate, or ill-fitting? → Look for other signs of either a free spirit or a general air of self-negligence.
- Do they constantly wear shoes that do not match the occasion? → Become curious about what they value instead. Do they prioritize fashion over conformity or comfort? Would they rather be cold than ugly?

Remember, though, that you need to think about the type of shoes that people wear not just once or twice, but *most often*.

Consider also that a person who has an enormous wardrobe of very different shoes may value novelty and choice more than a person who literally wears the same pair every single day.

Finally, shoes have a way of telling you about the person someone wishes they could be. If you can, peek into someone's closet and notice if there's a difference between what the person wears every day and what they tend to buy again and again.

A woman who lives in worn-out ballet flats but keeps on buying sparkly stilettos is telling you something about how she sees herself—and what she is aspiring to. It's a point worth bearing in mind: not everyone sees themselves accurately!

It's in the Way You Walk

Werner Wolff, a German-born psychologist, did one of the first studies examining the connection between gait (the way people walk) and personality. How a person walks, including their speed and stride length, can speak volumes.

Everyone is different.

So is the way they walk!

It's even been suggested that the way a person walks can give clues about what they are trying to hide from the world. Again, none of this is rocket science, but it does require us to pause, pay close attention, and carefully analyze what we are observing.

If someone is a fast walker...
- They may be a hardworking, outgoing person.

- Fast walkers tend to be open-minded, extroverted, and conscientious.
- Go-getters and risk-takers walk fast.
- Fast walkers tend to be bolder than usual, energetic, and detail oriented.
- They may also be more stressed!

If someone walks slowly and takes short steps...
- It's more likely they're an introvert.
- Slow walkers tend to be more contemplative and keep to themselves.
- Most of the time, people who walk this way are calm and happy when they are by themselves.
- When there are a lot of people in a room, you might notice that this person tends to move into the background or away from the center of attention.

If someone's walking style is loose and relaxed...
- It shows that they like to live life on their own terms and at their own speed.
- They're not in a hurry to be anywhere but here and now.
- They're also not in a hurry to take orders.
- They're calm, happy, and sure of themselves inside and out, but won't fight for the spotlight or try to stay ahead of the crowd.

If someone usually takes long, quick strides...
- They probably have a healthy attitude about life.
- Covering a lot of ground when walking suggests competitiveness, focus, and a desire to get things done.

- People still like them even if they sometimes come off as a little cold.

If someone is always dragging their feet...
- It suggests an anxious personality prone to worry.
- People who walk this way are usually upset or sad.
- They can't pull away from things or thoughts that make them feel bad. They can't stay in the present moment very often.
- Potentially, they keep "dragging" around their past or worry about losing things or people they care about.

But once again, *context* and *baseline* make all the difference.

Notice how a person is walking *relative to* others in group or compared to how they normally walk.

Notice if they always want to walk side by side with others, dawdle, or want to be in front.

Notice how their walking style might suddenly change, and become curious as to *why*.

As with other body language, look for the *openness* or *closedness* of the body, look for dynamism (suggesting confidence, joy, etc.) and gesture.

➡ One way to think of walking is that it is like *a visual representation of the way a person thinks*.
➡ Describe their walk and you have described their cognitive processes. Are they confident,

relaxed, and easy thinkers? Are they always going somewhere rather than just stretching their legs? Are they walking like a queen or scuttling nervously along like a crab?

Observe a Person's Food Choices

Juliet Boghossian is a food behavior expert in Los Angeles and founder of the food behavior research firm Food-ology. According to her, a person's eating habits can tell you enormous amounts about their personality, priorities, values, and identity. And why wouldn't it be that way, considering that what and how we eat probably represents dozens of choices we each make every day?

Observe people's behavior around food and drink and you can infer a lot about their state of mind and the way they think of themselves and the world. According to Boghossian:

If someone eats slowly...
- They may like to be in charge.
- They know how to savor life.
- They are also sure of themselves, in control, and calm.

If someone eats quickly...
- They may be ambitious, goal-oriented, and open to new experiences, but they may also have a tendency to be impatient.
- Eating quickly can also suggest distraction and anxiety, so watch for other context clues.

If someone loves to try new food...

- You can safely assume that they are open-minded and curious, and that they may be a lot less judgmental than the average person.
- This willingness to move out of a comfort zone can signal creativity, maturity, a joyful disposition, or perhaps a tendency toward boredom.

If someone is picky about what they eat...

- This generally suggests discomfort and anxiety of some kind or other.
- It's no coincidence that picky eating is most commonly associated with children, who are still developing their sense of discipline, adventurousness, and trust in the world.
- A fussy eater may demonstrate fearfulness or lack of maturity, or they may be signaling a desire to control the external environment in an attempt to moderate themselves internally.
- On the other hand, a limited palette can also be a simple question of habit and background. So much of what we enjoy eating comes down to how we have been raised, our culture, our income, what is available to us, and what brings us the most joy. What can you infer about an adult who won't eat their vegetables or who only ever wants to eat cheese pizza? It could be poor discipline, bad habits, or a more serious aversion... or all of these. Gather more data and you will get a clearer picture!

If someone likes to eat one food at a time...

- They are the so-called "isolationists." These people eat all of one food before moving on to the next, and so on around the plate.

- They pay a lot of attention to details and always give things a lot of thought. Predictably, they may like to do only one task at a time.
- They may be conscientious, a little anxious, disciplined, or possibly "control freaks" who would prefer if life stayed neat and orderly.

As you're making your observations, become curious about *everything* you see:

- How are their table manners? Slurping and talking with their mouth full, or taking pains to be neat and delicate? (Remember that table manners vary greatly between cultures, so keep that in mind as well!)
- Are they comfortable eating in front of others?
- Are they very certain about their preferences, or do they find making a decision difficult?
- Do they order the same thing everyone else does?
- Do they order the cheapest or most expensive thing on the menu?
- Do they avoid complaining if given the wrong food?
- How do they treat the waiter?
- Do they offer to pay, or do they wait coyly for you to do it?
- Are they snobby and disparaging about the food?
- Are they consciously dieting and talking about food in combative terms?
- Do they whip out their phone for Instagram pics while their food gets cold?

- Do they take food off your plate, offer you a taste of theirs, or happily chat to the people at the next table?

As you can see, it's all grist for the people-reading mill. Eating is never a neutral activity. How, what, when, and why we eat reveals much about how we understand our place in the world, our overall attitude and approach to life, our priorities, and our blind spots.

Perhaps now you can see the rationale behind the business lunch meeting. It's not a social occasion, but an opportunity to mine the rich data that comes from observing people doing ordinary things.

In just a ten-minute snack break, you can observe:

- How a person walks
- Their voice—pace, pitch, timbre, volume, etc.
- Their facial expressions
- Their clothing choices
- Their posture, gestures, and the way they move
- The language they employ
- The literal words they say
- Their behavior towards food
- Even their attitude towards money and what that says about power, control, and status

It's a lot of information, but all this data really starts to mean something when it's put together and embedded properly in the environment from which it emerged.

Importantly, when making your observations, about food or anything else, *try to keep your own assumptions and values out of the picture*. What you are trying to understand is what a certain food behavior means to them, not to you.

They may tell you that they are a vegetarian, and you may assume this is because they care about animal welfare. You then start telling yourself a story about how compassionate and conscientious they are. In fact, they are vegetarian for the health benefits only, and primarily because it's doctor's orders—that paints a very different picture!

A big caveat here: Humans are judgmental. Yes, even us! But judgment can get in the way.

There is a whole world of signs and symbols out there, most of them attached to a "good" or "bad" label. But it's only when we drop this value judgment and become genuinely curious that we can start to understand what we're actually looking at.

The deeper you go, the more thorough your understanding becomes. If you are lazy and simply think, "That guy makes tea in the microwave. I bet he's some kind of psychopath," for example, then you are missing out on a whole universe of valuable information.

Summary:

- We can gain real insights into people's characters by observing their choices, their behavior, and the function of this behavior.

Functional behavioral analysis is about formulating a theory about the functional relationship between a person's behavior and their environment, and not just static personality traits. Their behavior function may be access, attention, escape, or sensory. We can also observe the antecedents and consequences of behavior to see what triggers and sustains it.

- Emotion and behavior are linked, and nonverbal communication provides us with a world of information about a person. Body language reveals emotions in a spontaneous, unconscious, and unintentional way. Don't just read an individual, but that individual's behavior and orientation within their environment. Look for unusual, mismatched expressions and how people respond to those around them.

- Develop emotional granularity, which is a broad and deep knowledge of many different shades of emotion, plus the ability to distinguish between them. Remember that emotions can be concealed; watching for transitions and responses may be more illuminating.

- A baseline is a set of nonverbal behaviors that a person shows when relaxed. Pay attention to different-for-them behavior and remember to always consider context. Baselining can also help you identify lies and deception. Establish a baseline when relaxed, add stress and observe, then ask the relevant question and watch what happens.

- Finally, consider clothing, shoes, gait, and food choices as an extension of body language. The way a person walks can tell you about how they think and their level of ambition and stress, clothing can signal identity and intention, and food choices tell you a lot about a person's values and background.

Section 3

Chapter 9: NLP and People's Meta-Programming

In NLP, or neurolinguistic programming, meta-programs are basically our "maps of reality."

These maps describe our style of...

- Thinking
- Feeling
- Sorting
- Valuing
- Choosing
- Perceiving

...and consequently, they affect how we behave.

It can be fascinating to learn more about your own mental models of the world, but meta-programs can also offer us a rich insight into how *other* people tick.

So how do meta-programs work?

Whenever a person encounters something in the world, they form an internal representation of that event (i.e., a program) within their own minds.

➡ *How* they do this depends very much on a larger organizing principle, i.e., their meta-programs.

The brain is a pattern-making machine and it loves to take shortcuts. One shortcut is to make a simplified model of what it experiences. But the key is that brains are completely unique in the patterns they see (and don't see!), the meaning they create, the things they find most important, and the shortcuts they make.

Luckily, these internal models, though invisible, reveal themselves in countless ways as a person interfaces with other people and the world at large.

➡ To fully understand someone's meta-program, we need only pay attention to their words, body language, and actions—these are reflections of the kind of mental representation that person is working with.

Example: You're riding a rollercoaster with three new friends. As you round the corner, you are surprised by a scary fake monster that jumps out at you. Everyone screams (you included). But you notice something interesting after that.

- Friend 1 immediately breaks out into laughter.
- Friend 2 gets a little angry and defensive.
- Friend 3 starts mocking and teasing Friend 2 for being a big baby.

It's a small observation, but this difference in the way your friends react to *the same stimulus* can tell you a lot about the internal mental maps they are working from.

You notice how they talk about this moment the next day.

- Friend 1 talks about the group and how much fun "we" had and how everyone enjoyed themselves.
- Friend 2 complains about the surprise being sprung on them with no warning and talks at length about how unfair it is, and how doubly unfair it is that Friend 3 is being mean to them.
- Friend 3 says how they can't wait to go back to test to see if it's as scary the second time around.

These differences in reaction are interesting because they reveal something about the hidden worldviews from which they emerge.

The first friend is showing you that they think of the world as a largely happy, non-threatening place, but also that they aren't that good at noticing when other people's experience is not the same as theirs.

The second friend is showing you that they think of themselves as something of a victim and have chosen to focus on those parts of a situation that they see as unfair or unjust.

The third friend seems to enjoy being a rebel and different from the rest of the group. Instead of being amused or insulted by the rollercoaster surprise, he's curious and seems to want to return to master the situation.

Kinds of Meta-Programs

People are complicated.

Though there may be predictable patterns, most of us are complex and usually show a blend of different meta-programs. The program can also change depending on:

- context,
- stress levels, or
- life stage.

Nevertheless, the more we understand how other people make sense of their world, the more we understand *them*.

This means we can communicate with them more easily, work with them, and speak their language in such a way as to get around any potential conflict or misunderstanding. Whether you want to create better rapport or simply adapt and adjust so you can work around people more successfully, this NLP theory can help.

A meta-program is not exactly the same as a personality type, but it's similar! That's because the mental program someone is running is precisely what allows them to form their own beliefs, perspectives, and opinions, and decides how they will organize meaning around their actions, their circumstances, and other people they encounter.

➡ Here's an important thing to note: A meta-program is never "good" or "bad." It's neutral.
➡ It comes down to a simple question: What is this person going to focus on, and what are they going to filter out of awareness?

None of us are omniscient, i.e., aware of everything.

Simply by being alive, we apply mental filters to the world (you included).

You could say that a person's way of doing this is unique to them and a prime determiner of their character. Rather than "good" or "bad," the only judgment we can really apply here is whether this frame of reference is *helping* or *hindering* the person from achieving their stated aims (and again, their aims will be determined by their values, not necessarily yours).

Let's look at five common meta-programs used by NLP practitioners (there are seven, but we'll only consider the most common ones here) so we can better understand how to identify and work with each.

NLP Meta Program 1—Toward or Away

This is a question of "pain or gain."

Simply:

- Does the person move *toward* something positive?
- Or *away* from something negative?

Tony Robbins, a popular NLP proponent, says,

> "All human behavior revolves around the urge to gain pleasure or avoid pain. You pull away from a lighted match in order to avoid the pain of burning your hand. You sit and watch a beautiful sunset because you get pleasure from the glorious celestial show as day glides into night."

"Toward" people are goal-oriented.

They prioritize well and know what they want in life, as well as how to put that desire front and center.

They are motivated to always move toward something out there, in the future. Possibilities are imagined to be positive—however, there is sometimes so much positivity that critical thinking can take a back seat.

They are the "movers" in Kantor's Social Dynamics Theory, and they're often playing the part of leader and instigator.

"Away" people are also motivated, but to get away from something.

They're not crystal-clear on what they want, but they know very well what they *don't* want!

Their focus on problems and potential obstacles makes them a bit of a stick in the mud, but on the other hand, they are more likely to anticipate snags and think more clearly and pragmatically about the future.

How can you tell who's who?

Listen closely when people get very passionate about something.

Are they excitedly talking about what they want and are striving for? Or are they passionately positioning themselves *against* something else?

> **Example:** Let's say a person wants to lose weight. Notice how they talk about this goal. Is it "I'm going to look so hot when I reach my goal weight," or is it

"If I don't turn my bad habits around, I'm going to kill myself"?

The difference can be subtle.

Someone might *say* they're goal-oriented, but listen closely to how those goals are worded.

- "I want to not be fat anymore" is an *away* goal.
- "I want to be thin" is a *toward* goal.

Big difference.

Here's how you talk to a "toward person":

- You need to get on their wavelength and speak so that you center their goal.
- If you're trying to convince them of something, focus on the long-term benefits and positive outcomes of what you're talking about, use expansive, inclusive body language, and look upward as though toward a bright future.
- To smooth over conflict with them, talk about the future and how things will be better then, and downplay what's already happened.

How do you connect with an "away person"?

- You need to frankly acknowledge the problem and be honest. The key with this type of person is to mobilize their focus on the problem. Don't let them get diverted by crises, but ask what can be done to fix things.
- If you wish to motivate them, you may even hold them responsible for fixing a problem. Elaborate on the kind of situation you want to avoid, on risk, and on body language gestures that suggest exclusion.

- If there's conflict, focus on what you're going to do to escape that conflict, rather than trying to smile and minimize—this might actually inspire them to dig their heels in!

Imagine that you yourself are primarily a toward person but you're talking to an away person. Because you understand this, you don't get frustrated with them being a stick in the mud about an exciting holiday you're planning together.

When they keep homing in on potential disasters while you'd like to enjoy picturing how much fun you'll have, you decide that you won't argue with them or say things like "Don't be so negative! It'll never happen."

Instead, you say, "Hm, maybe you're right about getting better travel insurance. Not having good coverage could be a nightmare. Could you shop around and find the best option for us?"

NLP Meta Program 2—External or Internal Frame of Reference

This "sort" basically depends on how a person sets their frame of reference:

- Do they base their standards on *themselves*?
- Or on *other people*?

Internal frame-of-reference people...

- Are perceptive and self-centered. Here, the term isn't meant as an insult, but rather to show that such a person makes choices based on their own emotions and ideas.

- They process the world "from the inside out."
- They must feel *personally* satisfied with their work or choice or they don't consider it valuable.
- Frequently, they give preference to their own intuitions and gut feelings over what others say they should think.

On the other hand, **external frame-of-reference people...**

- Concentrate on others and the value they assign to things.
- They care about other people's opinions because, for them, agreement, harmony, and consensus are precisely what give choices their value.
- This is the kind of person who is largely unclear about their thoughts, beliefs, and behaviors until they know what other people's are. They can easily imagine making a choice that is favored by the group whilst not necessarily valuing it themselves.

Robbins claims,

"Ask someone else how he knows when he's done a good job. For some people, the proof comes from the outside. The boss pats you on the back and says your work is great. You get a raise. You win a big award. Your work is noticed and applauded by your peers.

When you get that sort of external approval, you know your work is good. That's an external frame of reference. For others, the proof comes from inside. They 'just know inside' when they've done well."

External frame of reference people are often "followers" in Kantor's model—people who are happy to support and validate someone else's initiative, but not too interested in instigating their own.

How can you tell if a person's frame of reference is internal or external?

➡	Simply ask them what their opinion is on a slightly contentious topic.
➡	You are listening not for what their answer is, but how they arrive at and justify that answer.

Maybe they say,

- "Well, I was raised Catholic, and we were taught X."
- "You'd be an idiot not to believe X."
- "Most people think X."

Both these answers suggest they may be *external*.

Maybe they say,

- "Well, a lot of people have different ideas."
- "My personal feeling is X."
- "My intuition is that X."

These answers suggest someone who is more internal.

It's not just what people say that can reveal their orientation; their body language may hold some clues, too.

- For an internal type, body language may be tight, closed, and focused on the self.
- For an external type, body language will be broader, more open, and less focused on the person themselves.

Importantly, people can be internal or external while varying considerably in how much they actually conform to society's expectations, so don't let that fool you.

Example: A person may do what their family/work/culture tells them to, but actually resent the fact and see their actions as valueless. On the other hand, someone might appear to be a rebel or a black sheep, but deep down really crave societal approval—they're just bad at getting it!

So, don't look at actions alone, but at the way people express themselves. Their choices matter, but *how they explain and justify those choices* matters more.

To connect with the internal type, the way is clear:

- Bear in mind that their source of value and meaning is internal. That means you speak about their experiences, wants, desires, needs, opinions, and so on.
- Frame the picture with them in the center, and there will seldom be any conflict. You make it so that they are deciding for themselves independently.

- These people have their own internally driven criteria—understand what they are and speak to them by framing your speech in terms of "I" and "you" and saying things like "personally..." or "that's your choice."

To connect with the external type, you must do the opposite:

- Introduce your own ideas or discuss others' ideas and how they might be useful.
- You are painting a harmonious picture and suggesting how they ought to fit into that.
- You might invoke ideas such as duty, obligation, convention, law, tradition, authority, or even just fashion.

Think about a teacher who is trying to support the learning of two very different students.

The first one he knows is an internal type, so when he gives feedback, he frames the student's performance in individualistic terms and refers to goals the student has set and to *their* values and principles.

Where something is a problem, the teacher frames this problem as a violation of the student's own ethical code (even if the teacher doesn't agree with this code in the least).

However, in talking to another student who he knows is more external, he refers to their performance in relation to others in the class, to the teacher's own expectations or disappointments, and to the commonly held grade standards that determine that student's accomplishment.

In dealing with more serious problems, the teacher might even mention the fact that the student's parents have paid a lot of money for school fees and will be upset that their child is not performing.

NLP Meta Program 3—Options or Procedures

- Does the person enjoy choosing from many options?
- Or do they want to follow the set path already determined by the rules?

This meta-program is about the *degree of autonomy* a person prefers.

The options type will:

- Actively seek out novelty.
- Value thinking outside the box.
- Prefer to be spontaneous and improvisational.

The procedures type is not that thrilled with this approach and will:

- Use a tried-and-true method.
- Follow a path that has already been established.
- Value efficiency and productivity above being creative.

To connect with an options person, you need to give them more options!

- Keep questions open-ended so you are always inspiring them to think about how they would create their own procedure.
- If you can, try to throw something unexpected into the mix—these people can be good

problem-solvers if you gently direct their enthusiasm to all the possibilities around a current problem.

- Lean into their desire to sink their teeth into a complex problem.

For the procedure person, on the other hand, your communication focus will always be on the HOW and not the WHY.

To connect with a procedures person, you need to clarify and respect the procedure.

- They don't necessarily want to reinvent the wheel for every project; simply give them clear instructions that will help them get the task done as quickly as possible.
- Don't bother trying to convey the broader implications or get them to be enthusiastic— their lack of enthusiasm does *not* mean they won't work hard or well.
- Be mindful of time limits, boundaries, and protocol. You'll win points if you work to make things simpler and more streamlined.

But how do you know which type of person you're dealing with?

Pay attention to *how they react to being given any type of task.*

Do they immediately start "playing" and trying to invent something new and different? Do they start trying to make something novel or "explore the space"?

➔ They're an options thinker ("What CAN I do?").

Do they diligently get on with it and produce an efficient (if conventional) result? Do they ask what is ordinarily done and what has been done before?

➜ They're a procedures person ("What DO I do?").

Example: Imagine you're planning Christmas with family. Some of your family members are options people, so you know that when you talk with them about what they'll contribute to festivities, you inspire them by asking for fresh ideas or something new and different they can create. ("Maybe we could do something totally different with the tree this year? Why don't you come up with something unconventional?")

With procedures people, you do none of this; you choose the quickest, most straightforward thing, then give them clear instructions for how to achieve it.("So you're in charge of Christmas Eve dinner, which is traditionally fish pie. I'll send you a recipe.")

Tip: As you can imagine, procedures people often have external frames of reference, too. Bear this in mind as you're gathering data.

NLP Meta Program 4—Matcher or Mis-matcher

The key difference here is about the attitude to relationships:

- Does someone focus on *differences* in relationships (mis-matcher)?
- Or do they focus on *similarities* (matcher)?

Matchers are focused on whatever overlap exists between them and another person.

They're:

- Optimistic and approving.
- Focused on finding *commonalities* in conversations.
- All about harmony and cohesion.

Thus, matchers base their decisions on similarities in others, circumstances, and life in general. They are always looking for the common denominator and value harmony and cooperation—which they may seek even to a fault.

The mis-matchers take a different strategy:

- Overall, they prefer to rebel, focusing on and amplifying differences.
- Their tendency to be oppositional can sometimes manifest as creativity, quirkiness, or insightful critical reasoning.
- The downside? It becomes fault-finding and general disagreeableness.

This is the kind of person who will automatically argue with you in a heated conversation, even if they don't actually have a strong opinion either way. They just like to identify a point of contention and lean into it.

Remember the "opposer" role in Kantor's model from earlier? The player whose actions worked in opposition to whatever initiative the "mover" was trying to initiate?

There is a big overlap between this meta-program and the pattern followed by the opposer.

Sometimes their opposition feels playful and generative.

Sometimes their questions or criticisms make a pretty good point.

Sometimes they make things feel like a competition... or a war.

Tony Robbins believes there are two subtypes of mis-matchers:

> "One type looks at the world and sees how things are different... The other kind of mis-matcher sees differences with exceptions."

Here, it's a question of what is seen first: Some people start with all the ways things are different, and then they build on to that the similarities. Others start with what is common and then look for exceptions.

➜ In both cases, the way to determine which type someone may be is to pay attention to *how they classify and perceive objects.*

Example:

Someone looks at a series of different-sized circles and notice one pertinent fact about them: "They're all circles."

That person is likely a *matcher*.

Someone else might immediately zoom in on what makes each of those circles different: "They're all different sizes."

That person is likely a *mis-matcher*.

Listen carefully if a person uses a lot of words that suggest difference:

- But
- Although
- However

Notice comparative language ("smaller" or "bigger") and notice if they are constantly defining themselves and their needs in opposition: "I'm *not* that way, I *don't* agree, I *can't* imagine that . . ." This grammatically negative language is a linguistic cue to how they see the world.

With a little practice, you can easily hear the match/mismatch difference of orientation in the way people speak.

Consider:

- Are they focusing on what is the same or on what is different?
- Are they amplifying distinctions or glossing over them?
- Are they zooming in on the one tiny thing you two don't agree on? Or are they quite quick to round everybody up into the same category and look for common ground—even if there may be very little?

Once you know a person's predominant type, you can speak to them in a way that will instantly build rapport and understanding.

To connect with the matching type:

- Lean into their tendency to find connections, and let them do the work—it's easy to find rapport with such a person since they will default to seeing you as similar to themselves.
- You can amplify their tendency by mirroring—use similar language, spoken metaphors, gestures, etc. to cement your harmony.
  - "What are we going to do about this?"—the use of *we* comfortably implies similarity and cooperation.

If you try to do this with a mis-matcher, though, you will actually inspire the opposite reaction in them. That's what they're all about—opposites!

Like many parents of rebellious teenagers know, you can go a long way with a little reverse psychology.

- Don't strain yourself trying to find common ground or persuade them into being more cooperative than they can be. Remind yourself that a mis-matcher isn't necessarily being unfriendly or combative.
- If it's a given that they'll push against and disagree with whatever you propose, then propose the opposite of what you want them to do or see.
  - "Now, I'm pretty sure you're going to shoot this idea down, but what about if we . . .?"
  - Here, you are working with the mis-matcher's tendency to immediately respond, "You're actually wrong on that. I *wouldn't* shoot it down. In fact, I think it's a great idea."

NLP Meta Program 5—Necessity or Possibility

Finally, notice how a person makes decisions.

- Are their decisions based on maximizing possibility?
- Or are their decisions more about satisfying necessity?

According to Robbins,

> "[Necessity people] are not pulled to take action by what is possible. They're not looking for infinite varieties of experience.
>
> They go through life taking what comes and what is available. When they need a new job or a new house or a new car or even a new spouse, they go out and accept what is available.
>
> Others are motivated to look for possibilities. They're motivated less by what they have to do than by what they want to do. They seek options, experiences, choices, paths."

For those more focused on necessity, there is a lot of value in "settling."

- They are happy to avoid the "bad thing."
- They don't necessarily value the process of endlessly looking around for alternatives and variety.
- For them, comfort and consolidation provide a lot of satisfaction.
- Enough really is… enough.

"Settling" has negative connotations in our culture, but getting comfortable with reality as you actually find it is a rational strategy. People who are able to cultivate contentment live more peaceful lives. And ironically, their satisfaction with life can put them in a better position to maximize on the opportunities that are actually available to them, instead of entertaining a bunch of pie-in-the-sky dreams.

The bad news? Necessity people may just as easily fail to venture out of their comfort zones, with underwhelming results. Stagnation is a risk.

What about those more focused on possibility?

- For people focused on possibility, there is plenty of excitement to be had in variety and opportunities for things to be different.
- They would prefer to pursue something enticing and unknown than to settle for the default.
- These are the people who take chances.
- Enough is just a baseline, and they are alert to what *more* they can get.

Both the advantage and disadvantage of this orientation is obvious: New and exciting ventures carry risks and costs, *sometimes enormous ones*, but also occasionally result in growth, which they highly prize. When things go wrong for possibility people, however, there is the *possibility* of them going spectacularly wrong.

How do we connect to a necessity person? To that person whose choices are about satisfying, not maximizing?

There's an art to it, especially if you're not a necessity person, or you're in a culture, work environment, or situation that prizes the other attitude.

- Firstly, remember that it's useless to focus on "what if"—this is not exciting for such a person. It may even be intimidating or unsettling.
- Instead, look at what *already is* and focus on the positives that are there.
- The idea is to amplify feelings of familiarity, security, ease, and safety.
- Find reasons for why the choice already made was a good one, rather than asking what choices could be made in the future.

A possibility person has a completely different motivation, so when you are attempting to communicate with them, you need to more heavily favor *what could be* rather than *what is*.

- Frame any course of action in terms of its future potential.
- Be aware that reminding them to be grateful, content, or satisfied will seldom do anything to motivate or interest them. Encouraging them to embrace what is already achieved may just leave them feeling flat, uninspired, or even a little sad.
- Don't be afraid to lean into challenge. Spur them to make plans.
- Steer questions toward growth, development, exploration, and novelty.

In a way, the split between necessity and possibility is the divide between conservative and progressive (in the psychological, not the political sense).

➜ Focusing on the benefits of staying the same (i.e., conserving) will leave possibility people uninspired and unconvinced, but will appeal to necessity types.

➜ The opposite is true: focusing on the benefits of change (i.e. progressing) will aggravate necessity types, but fire up possibility types.

How can you tell which type a person is?

Ask them any kind of "why" question.

For example:

"Why do you want to be a dental hygienist?"

"Why did you choose to live in this neighborhood?"

"Why did you decide on this particular restaurant?"

Then listen to the kind of answer you're given (important—not the content of the answer, but the way this content is framed).

- Do they frequently use language along the lines of "need" and "have to"? Do they rationalize their choice in terms of consolidation? Then they are likely operating from necessity:
  - "I was in a hurry and needed a qualification that I could earn in two years."
  - "We had to be near the school."
  - "Well, with this place, you know what you're getting."
- If they answer with language more to do with "want," or if they rationalize their choices as a way to optimize, then they are likely running the possibility meta-program:
  - "We wanted to be closer to nature."
  - "I was itching for a challenge."

○ "I just wanted to try something new, and see what happens…"

As before, listen for other meta-programs—this one overlaps predictably with the *away* and *toward* meta-program.

Now, knowing all this about each of the meta-programs, it's worth bearing in mind that it takes some skill to identify these models in others. Not least because you have a meta-program, too, and will be seeing others through *your* filter!

Always remember three important things about meta-programs:

- They are context-dependent
- They are stress-related
- They may change over time

So, don't observe a single event and assume you know everything about the person. Instead, notice *stable and recurring patterns*.

One thing to ask yourself: "What are my intentions?"

You need to clearly understand your own goal relative to this person.

Do you simply want to understand them better?

➜ Then work *with* and *inside* their meta-program, and don't oppose it.

Are you trying to communicate well and establish rapport?

➜ Then remind yourself that it is not your job to challenge, diagnose, or convince.

Are you trying to negotiate or resolve conflict?

➜   You may need to be a little strategic and frame your own ends in terms they'll easily understand.

Understanding your own meta-program will help you make changes, but unless you're a therapist or a motivational speaker, there's seldom a need to enter social interactions with the agenda of changing people's fundamental perspectives. In fact, bedding down into the mis-matcher meta-program yourself is the quickest way to arouse mistrust and resistance!

Finally, always keep in mind that the meta-program theory is about context and relativity.

People do not exist in a vacuum.

Their mental models are not static.

You may discover, once you're "out in the field," that there are many more varieties and variations on the programs listed here. That's OK. Notice how they are interacting with their environment and with other people, and how their meta-programs, whatever they are, are actually functioning.

In other words, if you want to quickly understand how someone ticks, ask what function their mental model is actually serving.

➜   **People think the way they do for a reason.**
➜   **So, what's the reason?**

Look at the way they respond to other people, to challenges, to opportunities, to ambiguity, etc. Look at the choices they make and the stories they tell about those choices. Even pay attention to what they're *not* saying.

All of this will tell you a lot about the invisible mental programming they're running.

Summary:

- Meta programs are our mental maps or representations of reality. We need only pay attention to people's words, body language, and actions to infer the meta-programs they are running. Most people show a blend of different programs and can change over time.
- Identify the meta-program and then work with it to create harmony and understanding, remembering that meta-programs are contextual, relative, and influenced by stress.
- One program is whether they move *toward* something positive or *away* from something negative. Observe what people are passionate about and how they frame their motivations.
- Another program is *external* versus *Internal* frame of reference—i.e., whether a person bases their standards on themselves or on others. To test this, ask questions about the person's source of value or satisfaction, or ask their opinion on a slightly contentious topic, and observe how they justify and explain their choice.
- Discern between *options* versus *procedure* thinking—i.e., the degree of novelty, autonomy, and spontaneity a person prefers. To tell the difference, pay attention to how a person reacts to being given a task.

- Discern between *matchers* and *mis-matchers*—i.e., whether someone focuses on similarities or differences. Observe the way they classify and group objects—is it according to similarities or differences?
- Finally, discern between *necessity* or *possibility* mindsets—i.e., are they maximizing or simply satisfying? Ask a "why" question and listen for "need to" versus "have to" clues.

Chapter 10: The Art of the "Soft Probe"

So far, we've covered a lot of theoretical ground.

- We've explored the four basic personality types.
- We've experimented with "perceptual positions" and what switching between them can reveal to us.
- We've learned to take a functional view of behavior.
- We've learned to read emotions—and compare what we see against baseline.
- We've broadened our observation to include things like clothing, gait, and food choices.
- Finally, we've explored the major "meta-programs" and some ways we can tell what program a person may be running.

Simply knowing all this information is going to change the way you approach people.

The way you listen to them.

What you see.

What you hear.

But in this chapter, we're going to deliberately kick things up a notch.

We want to move from passive reading to active reading.

What's the difference?

- Passive reading:
  - You're observing what unfolds in front of you.

- o You're analyzing, synthesizing and interpreting that data.
- o You're coming to a conclusion about that person.
- Active reading:
- o You're doing all of the above.
- o You're also *actively engaging in the moment* with the person as you read them.
- o You're making and testing hypotheses in real time.

Active reading is richer, almost "three dimensional."

It's the art of using low-stakes testing to verify your theories and hypotheses about someone right there, as you interact with them. This thinking on your feet, making real-time adjustments of your working model of a person, as you talk to them.

It's free form and ad hoc, but that doesn't mean there is no structure or strategy involved.

Let's take a closer look.

The SUE Framework

Par Anders Granhag is Professor at the Institute of Psychology at the University of Gothenburg, Sweden. He and his fellow researchers are interested in the art of "eliciting critical information."

To you and me, that means discovering:

- Clever interrogation strategies.
- New ways to detect deception in interviews.

- Efficient techniques for convincing perpetrators "in denial" to reveal important information about their crimes (Tekin et. al., 2015; Granhag et. al., 2007).

It's exciting stuff, but can it help us become better people-readers?

Let's first explore what Granhag calls the SUE framework—Strategic Use of Evidence.

→ Insight: *The way* an interviewer reveals what they know has a big impact on what the interviewee reveals.
→ Strategy: "Information elicitation" is most effective when the interviewer withholds certain known facts to see if the subject's "free narrative" contradicts them.

This is where the "use of evidence" comes in—evidence here being crucial information or known facts. Gradual or delayed disclosure of information gives a strategic advantage.

How?

The general idea is to pay attention to *timing*:

- The interviewer starts with a free-form narrative.
- They encourage the interviewee to tell *their* story in the same free-form way.
- The interviewer then gradually asks more and more specific and targeted questions. These questions act as a "funnel" towards the facts the interviewer already knows.
- The interviewer listens very carefully to the interviewee's story.

- Here's the important part: The interviewer then looks for *discrepancies between what he already knows and what the interviewee is telling him.*

If the interviewer reveals what he knows too early, the interviewee can simply adjust and say whatever they think they need to. Consciously or unconsciously, they will try to reconcile what the interviewer telling them with their own story—and that muddies the waters.

But by withholding that information, the interviewer is creating an opportunity for the interviewee to reveal themselves—to show their hand.

Liars and truth-tellers tell stories in different ways.

In the same way, people operating from different meta-programs will tell stories in different ways.

→ The less of your own story that you inject into the picture, the more clearly you will see *their* story—and the more you'll learn.

This way, you are probing "softly"—sometimes even appearing like you're not probing at all!

As it happens, the SUE technique is empirically proven to be effective at deception-detection, specifically because it forces deceivers to produce discrepancies—which immediately reveals the lie.

For our purposes, we're less concerned with spotting deception, and more interested in finding out how people think.

Who they are.

What they want.

The SUE framework provides a *strategy* and a *structure* that we can co-opt to become more active people-readers.

A few principles we can borrow from the world of interrogation science:

- People don't spontaneously "confess." We cannot accept what we're told at face value. We cannot make assumptions.
- We need to have a continually running hypothesis that we test as we go. We start with what we know for sure, then build on that, gradually revealing the truth one step at a time.
- Use the "baseline" principle, where the baseline is the fact/truth you already know, and the deviation from that baseline is the story they're telling you, and how they're telling it.
- The less you say—the less you "lead" with questions and assumptions—the less chance they'll have to tailor their presentation to suit their own agenda.

In practice, here's the form the SUE framework takes:

- ➡ Clarify certain topics or events for which you have the facts.
- ➡ Encourage people to tell their story by asking open-ended questions that funnel the conversation towards the facts you have.
- ➡ Compare *your facts* with *their story*.
- ➡ Look for discrepancies.

→ Now, interpret. What do those discrepancies tell you? Do they help you confirm or disconfirm your current hypothesis?

Example: You're trying to learn more about a new acquaintance.

Working hypothesis: Currently, you believe that they are running the necessity meta-program, the external frame of reference meta-program, and they may be more of a matcher than a mis-matcher.

One day, a mutual friend Jack tells you that he's had a car accident and is in the hospital. You offer to visit him, but he declines and tells you that he doesn't want any visitors. He mentions that he is overwhelmed and has asked all friends and family not to come, and instead to give him some space.

Facts: You know that Jack has asked people not to visit him.

Now, the next day you are chatting to your new acquaintance, and they mention that they heard Jack was in the hospital. You encourage them to talk.

They tell you:

"Poor Jack, he's having such a hard time! I have to go and visit him this afternoon."

As a funnel question leading towards the facts you already possess, you ask casually:

"Oh, did he ask you to come?"

The acquaintance replies:

"Well of course I'll go, I have to. It's just what you
do for friends."

Can you see it?

- The clue words: "Have to" and "must."
- The discrepancy: "I have to go" vs. Jack has
  specifically refused visitors.
- There is definitely evidence here for this
  person running the matcher, necessity, and
  external meta-programs!

You are learning something *very* interesting about
your acquaintance—that their guilt-obligation-duty
meta-program is so strong it can actually override
the facts of the situation, i.e. that poor Jack has
asked to be left alone.

This is a person who is using the necessity "sort" to
make sense of their reality, and basing their
decisions on an external frame of reference (saying
"It's just what people do," and not "It's what *I* want
to do.")

The magic of the SUE framework is that it invites
people to actual show you, in real time, how they
piece together their worlds.

The assumptions they're making.

The interpretations they're bringing.

You don't have to be a detective. Just listen and lead.
Gently encourage them to talk, and most people will
willingly unfold their meta-programs for you.

*Behavioral Confirmation and the Problem With
Presuming Guilt*

In quantum physics, the "observer effect" describes how the mere act of measuring or observing a system is enough to actually change the system, thereby changing what is observed and measured.

The same is true in behavioral science: there is no real way to be "neutral" in a social system, no way to simply be an observer in a conversation or interaction.

Simply by being present in the system, we change that system!

A study by Kassin et. al. (2003) showed that an interviewer's expectations (their "hypothesis") influence their questioning style, and that in turn actually changes the interviewee's behavior.

The interviewer then observes the very behavior he anticipated.

→ This phenomenon is called "behavioral confirmation" because the interviewee behaves in a way that *confirms* the expectations and assumptions of the interviewer.

Kassin et. al.'s research was structured like this:

"52 suspects guilty or innocent of a mock theft were questioned by 52 interrogators led to believe that most suspects were guilty or innocent. Interrogators armed with guilty as opposed to innocent expectations:

- Selected more guilt-presumptive questions.
- Used more interrogation techniques.
- Judged the suspect to be guilty.

- Exerted more pressure to get a confession—particularly when paired with innocent suspects" ("Behavioral confirmation in the interrogation room: on the dangers of presuming guilt", *Law and Human Behavior*).

In the second part of the study,

"Neutral observers listened to audiotapes of the suspect, interrogator, or both. They perceived suspects in the guilty expectations condition as more defensive—and as somewhat more guilty."

The implications are obvious:

"A presumption of guilt sets in motion a process of behavioral confirmation by which expectations influence the interrogator's behavior, the suspect's behavior, and ultimately the judgments of neutral observers."

While fascinating, studies like this should give us pause.

→ Our *expectations* are powerful.
→ Our *assumptions* have the capacity to actually distort and influence reality.

We need to be exceedingly careful here.

- The idea is to carry a temporary hypothesis, NOT a foregone conclusion.
- Our questions need to be explorative and open-ended, NOT assumptive.
- We should always be testing a working model, NOT looking for confirmation for it.

If you expect someone to be a mis-matcher, for example, you may accidentally provoke them into actually being one!

Remember: You are never truly observing someone as they are. You are observing them as they are *in your company.*

Keep this in mind and never forget that your presence, your expectations, and your assumptions exert their own influence on what is unfolding.

So, how do you probe without "leading the witness?"

As you listen, you're keeping your ears pricked for the mental filters—the evidence of different meta-programs in action.

You're listening for clue words.

So far, so good.

However, when we move from passive to active people-reading, we do need to be aware of the increased risk of bringing our own confirmation bias to the table.

One quick way to lessen that risk?

➜ Be aware of how you use the "statement-as-question."

This is a subtle but powerful distinction to understand.

Let's say you suspect someone of running the mis-matcher meta-program.

You hypothesize that they have a tendency to focus on differences in social situations, to rebel, and to frame things in terms of opposition.

Here's what you might say to them:

- **Statement**: "We make a good team."
- **Question**: "Do you think we make a good team?"
- **Statement-as-question**: "We make a good team, don't we?"

Now, on the face of it, there doesn't seem to be too much difference between these three.

But the delivery makes all the difference!

Let's take a closer look.

A question is very obviously a question. It demands an answer.

A statement, similarly, poses itself as something that someone has to react to—to either agree with or disagree with, confirm or disconfirm.

But the statement-as-question hits differently, psychologically speaking. It's gentler. More subtle.

It's not really stating anything, neither is it really asking anything.

It just poses a potential reality.

Then lets it just... *hang there.*

Let's look at the response that each one might receive.

"We make a good team, don't we?"

- A matcher will readily and happily agree. They may skim over this statement, simply because they take it as a given.
- A mis-matcher, however, will react to this completely differently. They may quietly scoff, raise their eyebrows, chuckle awkwardly, frown, scowl, or say something jokey or sarcastic. Whatever it is, it's *not* the ready and happy agreement the matcher will provide.

However, if you had led with a statement or question, you may have received a much less revealing and informative response.

"We make a good team."

- Both matchers and mis-matchers may simply keep quiet. One because they agree, the other because they *don't* agree! Either way, people are much less inclined to have readable reactions to plain statements like this.

"Do you think we make a good team?"

- A matcher will say *yes*, and a mis-matcher likely won't, so a question in this case may be useful.
- But questions are much less useful when testing for the other meta-programs.
  - **Example:** Someone is both a matcher and favors options over procedures. If you asked them, "Are you getting on well with your new supervisor?" they may say *yes* (because they're a matcher and want to confirm the assumption hidden in your question), but quietly think *no* (because they're options

people, and they hate being forced to follow external rules).

o   Your question is therefore a *leading one*. It produces confirmation bias and yields precisely zero useful information!

All of this is simply to say that our questions matter, and the *form* of our questions matters, too.

As a rule of thumb:

- **Statements** tend to shut things down. They do not invite the other person to unfold their narrative in a way that yields interesting information for you to read.
- **Questions** tend to lead and influence. They make it clear what your assumptions and expectations are, and lead the other person down a particular path.
- **Statements-as-questions** are somewhere in the middle. They probe without seeming to probe. They make tentative statements and ask questions without suggesting the desired answer.

Remember that you can turn a statement into a statement-as-question simply by changing the tone of your voice, or slightly shifting the wording:

"You're leaving on Tuesday" completely changes if you simply elevate your pitch at the end of the sentence → "You're leaving on Tuesday?"

Consider also:

"You're leaving on Tuesday, hm?"

"You're leaving on Tuesday, aren't you?"

Finally, there's one foolproof way to make sure that your questions are not having an influence on the answers you're getting:

Stay genuinely open-minded.

→ **Remember:** If you don't actually hold any expectations, assumptions, or foregone conclusions about someone, it's impossible for any confirmation bias to occur!

Say less.

Listen more.

Don't reveal everything that you know all at once.

Test, probe, and compare.

Have a hypothesis, *but hold it lightly.*

Chapter 11: Keep Your Ears Pricked for Word Clues

If you want to know who people are, simply listen—they will *tell* you!

No, they will seldom spell it out directly, but if you know how to "listen between the lines," there is a whole world of insight you can glean from a person's ordinary speech.
Some word choices in particular reveal interesting things about the person who chose them. John Schafer, an FBI behavior analyst, called these especially revealing words Word Clues.

By looking at the words people use when they talk or write, Word Clues help you:

- Understand what motivates people
- Predict how they will behave
- Gain a deeper understanding of how they see their world

Of course, Word Clues can't tell you *everything* about a person's personality, but they can give you a good starting point. Word Clues are a great way to come up with an initial hypothesis about someone. With more in-depth observations, you can then test this hypothesis and gradually confirm your original hunches.

All you have to do is

- Listen carefully
- Identify certain words
- Make educated guesses about what these word choices suggest, in context

Here's the key parts of Schafer's theory:

→ When people think, they do so using only verbs and nouns.
→ Other parts of speech—adjectives and adverbs, especially—are added on purpose after the fact.
→ *Why* they are added reveals something about the speaker, what they are trying to achieve, and why.

If you simply notice adjectives and adverbs in everyday speech, you will more readily notice this form of bias that people can't help but reveal.

Example: Imagine someone tells you, "A black man killed that beautiful young woman." You'd instantly wonder *why* the adjectives "black," "young," and "beautiful" were included, right?

A more subtle example: Imagine someone is telling you an anecdote, and they say at some point, "I walked quickly." You notice this word "quickly" and how it's not really an integral part of the meaning of the story.

The person is telling a story about something else entirely, but they add in this tiny detail about how quickly they walked to get to the train and arrive at a meeting.

"Quickly" becomes a Word Clue for you.

It gives a sense of urgency, but it doesn't explain *why* the urgency is there.

Let's think. *You* might walk quickly because you're afraid of being late to a meeting, and you're conscious of the disappointment that comes with breaking a social norm like being on time.

But what does "walk quickly" mean to *them*?

- Perhaps, given the context and what you know of this person, it might suggest that they wish to be thought of as reliable and trustworthy.
- Perhaps it matters to them to live up to expectations.
- Perhaps the word implies a more general sense of anxiety and heightened tension. "Quickly" can suggest haste, even a tiny bit of fear.

Either way, the fact that the person has included this Word Clue in a story that isn't actually about time tells you something.

What does it tell you? Well, the rest of the conversation will help you decide.

But what's important is that your observation is a *clue*—not a full-blown conclusion about anything, just a clue.

A hint.

A suggestion.

If you find several other such hints and suggestions in the person's speech, you gradually get to confirm one of your original hypotheses.

For example, if the person uses lots of other adverbs to suggest promptness, correctness, and reliability (even when these details are not crucial to the story at hand) then you can be sure that you are dealing with someone who is conscientious, eager to please, and observant of social etiquette.

The next time you're talking with someone, tune out the content for a moment and listen to the word choices they are making.

1. Identify the core, necessary parts of speech—verbs and nouns
2. Identify everything else
3. Then ask what this "everything else" means—why was it chosen and not something else?

Example: Your aunt arrives at your house unannounced one day. She says to you, "Oh, I'm sorry. I was in the neighborhood, so I thought I'd just come over for a teeny tiny visit. Hopefully you still like almond cookies, right?"

OK, let's break this down:

The core of this piece of communication is: "I came to visit."

Everything else is extra:

- The fact that she is *sorry.*
- She's aware that you won't like her coming unannounced.

- She gives a reason for her visit (being in the neighborhood).
  - o She feels it necessary to justify her visit.
- The fact that she *just* came over for a *teeny tiny* visit.
  - o This adverb and adjective combination suggests she doesn't want to intrude, but she's downplaying the inconvenience she might be causing.
- She has brought cookies expressly for you, and *hopefully* you *still* like them.
  - o "Hopefully" suggests that they are a kind of offering to offset showing up unannounced, and the "still" carrying all sorts of connotations—it implies that she has known you for a long time, that she is familiar with your tastes. She is pointing subtly to a shared history and bond.

Can you see how the bulk of what your aunt is really saying is *outside* of the main components of the message itself?

All you need to do to confirm this is to change these extra details while keeping the central message intact, noticing how much it changes everything:

➜ "I've brought you some almond cookies. Well, are you going to invite me in? Or is the place a mess?"

Or what about:

➜ "Hello, hello, hello! It's your favorite aunt! Surprise! You are going to just die when you see what I've brought for you."

Of course, you'd be exhausted if you had to analyze every sentence out of every person's mouth, but it is good to remember that nothing that people say or do is ever really *neutral*.

Remind yourself that people are often in the position of being able to say absolutely anything at all, but they choose one specific thing.

Why?

Answering that question gives you a glimpse into their world.

For fun, let's look at a few more examples.

Example: "I won another award."

➔   Word Clue: "another."

This word choice not only makes the point that the speaker won previous awards, but also that they wish to draw your attention to this fact.

This person wants to ensure that other people know that he or she won at least one other award, thus bolstering his or her self-image. If you notice other corroborating Word Clues of this kind, you can safely conclude that this person needs or enjoys the adulation of others to reinforce their self-esteem.

- Want to exploit this vulnerability? Use flattery and other ego-enhancing comments.
- Want to connect more deeply with such a person? Understand that their self-worth is a tender point, but a potential inroad to more authenticity in future communication with them.

Example: "I worked hard to achieve my goal."

➜   Word Clue: "hard."

All achievements require work. But if someone emphasizes the *hardness* of the work, what does it imply?

The Word Clue "hard" may suggest a few things:

- They may value goals that are difficult to achieve, precisely because of their difficulty. They may relish a challenge, seeing its difficulty as proof of the value of any action.
- They may wish to emphasize how much they personally deserve that outcome, suggesting a kind of pride or even entitlement.
- They may feel a little defensive or even accusatory. You can almost imagine this line following an unspoken sentence: "I know others get things in life for free, but... I worked *hard* for this."

Finally, listen for other Word Clues, since other interpretations are possible. For example, someone may say this a few times specifically to emphasize that it was not luck or talent that won, but sheer grunt work.

They may have a strong desire to be recognized for their work, or even for others to admire them or acknowledge the sacrifices they made.

Compare the following two pairs of statements and notice how, in context, the Word Clue "hard" suggests different interpretations.

- "Growing up, I had none of the support you kids have today. I worked hard to achieve my goal."
- "I know some people find a bachelor's degree a walk in the park, but I don't care. I worked hard to achieve my goal."

See the difference context makes?

Example: "I patiently sat through the lecture."

➜ Word Clue: "Patiently."

Another adverb that tells a story.

The Word Clue "patiently" points to a kind of problem that requires bearing with.

- Perhaps this person is bored with the lecture.
- Maybe they don't think very highly of the lecturer.
- Maybe they think very highly of their own mastery of the subject.

Regardless of the reason, this person is preoccupied with something other than the content of the lecture... and yet chose to stay in the lecture. Furthermore, they want to *tell* you about this discrepancy.

Note, they don't say "I went to the lecture." They are communicating something additional with the Word Clue "patiently."

What could it be?

Perhaps this is a person who adheres to social norms and etiquette but doesn't especially like doing so and wants you to know that while they'll follow certain rules, that doesn't mean they like them! After all, a person who doesn't care about social rules will just leave a lecture if they're not enjoying it. They will not present this action as something out of the ordinary, either.

So what does it mean if a person does frame a situation this way?

Let's say you form the hypothesis: "This person is externally motivated. They're fair and law abiding, but a little passive."

Later, you notice again that they complain a few times about things they're uncomfortable with, but you also notice they make no efforts to improve the situation or get away from it in any way. This kind of thing is subtle but powerful—you are noticing that this person has an external locus of control.

So what?

Well, people with external loci of control are those who tend not to take responsibility for their own lives, but who see occurrences, good or bad, as always stemming from other people or circumstances, and not of their own volition. This is a pretty good thing to know when it comes to choosing a running partner to keep you accountable to your fitness commitments, right?

You can predict that this is the kind of person who will avoid a workout and then blame something or someone else.

Example: "I did the right thing."

→   Word Clue: "Right."

The focus is not on the thing that was done. Neither is it on *why* it was done. Instead, this clue word alerts you that, for the speaker, there is an important moral dimension at play.

If this kind of framing turns up repeatedly, you may be talking to someone who:

- Has a sense of right and wrong that is currently front-and-center.
- May frame their own actions in terms of objective measures of truth (consider how this aligns with the internal vs. external meta-program).
- May even have experienced a recent ethical dilemma that they've overcome.
- Has gone through some level of internal or external opposition in order for them to arrive at their current position.
- May be experiencing some feelings of guilt or self-doubt.

If all this seems like a stretch, consider all the other possible ways the sentiment could be expressed:

- "I did what was right for me."
- "I did what I was supposed to."
- "I did what I did."

These meanings could not be more different, right?

A person who litters their speech with reference to goodness and rightness is, obviously, sending a message. It's not just that they hold personal values, but that they believe in some higher, objective ethical standards to which they align themselves.

In other words, you're probably dealing with a pretty trustworthy and scrupulous person!

Example: "It was done . . ."

Finally, listen for people who frequently use passive voice when they speak, rather than active voice.

This not a "Word Clue" as such, but a sentence structure that quietly acts to center either the actor or the action.

To quickly explain:

- The dog bit Johnny.
  - This is active voice
  - The dog is the agent or subject doing the action of biting.
- Johnny was bitten (by the dog).
  - This is passive voice.
  - The object, or recipient of the action (Johnny), is highlighted, while the subject—the dog—is missing or downplayed.

The way that people order the subject and the object in a sentence tells you a lot about their perceptions around:

- Culpability
- Agency
- Choice

The first sentence centers the dog and very clearly identifies it as the agent who did an action—biting.

The second sentence, however, puts Johnny in the center, and the dog becomes less important, or even invisible.

→ The way we frame action points to the story we want to tell, and what we want to claim is most important.

In the second sentence, what matters more is that someone was bitten, not *who* did the biting.

When listening for this, the idea is not simply to identify active or passive voice. Instead, it's to understand *why* that voice has been chosen, and what this tells you about the intention and perspective of the speaker.

Example: Someone tells you, "I'm sorry you were hurt" when they could have just as easily said "I'm sorry I hurt you."

Why?

Usually, passive voice users are trying to downplay agency—likely their own.

They may be running an external reference meta-program and don't truly see themselves as responsible or to blame. This distinction goes beyond just the grammatical fact of passive voice, though.

Compare:

* "We arrived at the party."
* "I took us to the party."

The latter is more concerned with the agency and actions of one specific person than the action itself. If a person is repeatedly talking about themselves this way, you can infer that they see themselves in the driver's seat (in this case, literally!) and that this is the most salient feature of this situation for them.

A final word of warning here: While FBI agents and interrogators often have to come to life-or-death conclusions based on very little information, you can give yourself more leeway.

No single Word Clue is enough on its own.

- Look for recurring patterns and choices.
- Look for clusters of behaviors that reinforce a hypothesis.
- Look for the broader meaning these choices convey about the person who chose them and not some other words.

Listening to Tone of Voice

As the old saying goes, it's not what you do, it's the way that you do it.

Or to put it another way, it's not what you say, it's the way you say it.

➔ A person's tone of voice may be one of the most meaningful components of what they're communicating to you.

Consciously or unconsciously, people convey enormous amounts of information in their voice, through:

- Timbre
- Speed
- Clarity
- Tone
- Pitch
- Volume
- Articulation

- Projection

And we can read this information despite the words they are or aren't saying!

If a dozen people all say the same sentence, they'll each do it in a completely unique way, and their different tones of voice will tell you a lot about their different psychological states (not to mention the differences in accents and voice "age"—but that's for another chapter).

The Laboratory of Instrumental Analysis of Communication at the Autonomous University of Barcelona conducted a research study investigating tone of voice and perception. Their findings were fascinating.

They discovered that deeper voices were associated with maturity, while higher tones were perceived to carry less credibility. However, extremely deep voices could go too far and convey something more sinister. Talking very quietly was perceived as weak or unconfident.

The big question here is, if we perceive these things to be true, does that mean they're *actually* true?

While there probably are socialized and arbitrary elements (for example, it wouldn't be fair to say that women, who have naturally higher-pitched voices, are all uniformly less credible than men, who have naturally lower voices), we can nevertheless make some educated guesses about the variations in voice that are *not* genetic and unchangeable.

Breath

Voice is made out of breath.

How someone speaks comes down to their mastery and regulation of air flow from the lungs over the vocal cords.

- If someone's voice is calm and even → it's likely they feel calm and even, too.
- A person who speaks as though they're constantly running out of air → this tells you that they are nervous, unsure, or rushed.
- A choked or tight voice → muscular tension often hints at psychological tension!

Volume

How loud we speak conveys plenty of information about how much "aural space" we are comfortable taking up. This in turn speaks volumes (pardon the pun) about confidence and visibility.

- People who talk loudly or even over others (or screaming babies, for that matter) are sending a clear message that they feel confident and even entitled to dominate the airwaves.
- A person talking quietly, though, isn't always telling you that they're timid or unconfident. Some other possibilities include:
- This is an extremely strong and self-assured person; they feel no *need* to shout for attention. They feel confident they'll be heard.
- When someone whispers, they may be deliberately drawing us in closer to them so we

can hear—it's a power move. It signals, "*You* make effort to come to *me*."

o   For similar reasons, talking quietly can signal intimacy, a desire for intimacy, or outright seduction. After all, physical proximity suggests quieter voices, or perhaps the switch the more nonverbal modes of communication.

Articulation

When something is articulate, it has clear distinctions between its parts.

Think of vocal articulation in terms of *agility*, i.e., how much skill and dexterity there is in the way a person moves from one word to the next.

- Is the person talking with clarity, ease, and control? Is their voice moving with precision and proficiency?
- Or is their speech chaotic, imprecise, stumbling, inelegant, or filled with "ums" and "likes"?

Vocal mastery is almost always a reflection of some other form of mastery. Become curious about what that might be.

A person who is verbally articulate may be signaling that they are:

- intelligent,
- knowledgeable,
- experienced,
- well organized,
- confident,

- well-regulated, or
- on the ball in some other way (or, at least, they like to think so!).

Speed

Speed of speech tells you a lot about emotional state and degree of excitement.

- Is the speed slow and ponderous? This could mean that there's a lack of interest there, or even a disconnect. (It's important to see the source of this indifference, though—is it the topic being discussed, the audience, or life in general? Do they just not like *you*?)
- A rapid speed? This can suggest excitement, but also tension or a feeling of being rushed.
- An irregular speed? This suggests confusion on the part of the speaker, or that communication breakdown is occurring.

Pitch

Research by the University of Göttingen published in the *Journal of Research in Personality* suggests that a lower-pitched voice is associated with people who are:

- more dominant,
- extroverted, and/or
- more "sociosexual" (meaning they're more interested in casual sex or sex outside of a relationship).

They claimed these findings were true for both men and women.

The researchers asked two thousand people to complete personality tests and then analyzed recordings of their voices so that pitch could be measured objectively by computers.

According to research conducted by Dr. Julia Stern,

> "Even if we just hear someone's voice without any visual clues—for instance, on the phone—we know pretty soon whether we're talking to a man, a woman, a child, or an older person. We can pick up on whether the person sounds interested, friendly, sad, nervous, or whether they have an attractive voice. We also start to make assumptions about trust and dominance."

Stern's research shows that we may be right to make these assumptions after all!

An easy tip to learning to read people's tone of voice is to simply become more aware of your own. After all, you always know how *you* feel in situations; pay attention to how this manifests in your voice. What is true for you is probably true for others.

Here's a fun exercise to try:

Watch a movie, but in a language foreign to you.

- Listen closely to how the actors and actresses are speaking.

- Try to glean as much information from this as possible.
- To train yourself to focus on the sound alone, you could even close your eyes and completely remove the visual element.
- What can you guess about the way they are feeling just from the quality of their voices?
- Later, adding subtitles and rewatching can let you know how close you were!

Understand Function Words

Can pronoun use tell you anything about a person? According to James Pennebaker's research in the '90s, the answer is *yes*.

Pennebaker helped develop software that analyzed various texts, including student essays, instant messages, press conference transcripts, and more. This research revealed that "function words" give more important clues to a person's emotional state than "content words." In this context:

- Function words = pronouns, articles, prepositions, conjunctions, and auxiliary verbs.
- Content words = nouns, adjectives, verbs, adverbs.

According to Pennebaker,

"Function words help shape and shortcut language. People require social skills to use and understand function words, and they're processed in the brain differently. They are the key to understanding relationships between speakers, objects, and other people. When we analyze people's use of function words, we can get a sense of their emotional state and personality, and their age and social class."

Pronouns tell us where we have put our focus. Imagine you ask someone what the weather is. Consider these two possible answers:

1. It's hot.
2. I think it's hot.

That little extra pronoun in the second option seems small, but it makes a big difference.

It shows a focus on the self.

If you had a hunch that the person you were talking to had an internal frame of reference, this would certainly be a clue to support that hypothesis. Interestingly, Pennebaker found that depressed people use "I" more often than non-depressed people. Now that's something to listen out for!

Pennebaker also believes that people who are lying tend to use "we" more often, or even avoid first-person pronouns, almost as an unconscious bid to rope you in on the reality they're trying to sell you.

Those intending to deceive or obscure their culpability will often make generalized statements that include everyone else.

Example: They won't say, "I didn't take the money," but something like, "These days, everyone knows you can't just leave money lying around like that."

On the other hand, the repeated use of "we" in certain contexts could indicate a strong social bond—or the desire for/assumption of one.

People who heavily use articles (like "a," "an," and "the") are communicating a concrete style of thinking, i.e., they tend to see ideas, situations, and even people as things or objects in their field.

Conversely, people who tend to refer to things and situations in relational terms are telling you that they predominantly focus on relationships and dynamics between people.

Example: Compare the difference between "I'll bring my wife" and "I'll bring the wife."

It's important to state here that these findings were made using computer software to analyze very small differences in speech—in other words, variations that were too tiny to be perceived in ordinary interactions. In addition, they were applied to populations, not individuals.

That doesn't mean you can't use their insights in your own life to better read people; it just means that

you will need to clock many more repeated instances
of a particular language clue before you can conclude
anything meaningful.

How Language Reflects a Person's Meta-Program

You've probably noticed that there is significant
overlap in how we interpret Word Clues, tone of
voice, and function words, and how we analyze the
meta-program a person is running.

Let's say you're trying to determine if a person is
using the NLP meta-program of internal or external
reference.

You listen closely and the person drops Word Clues:

- "I chose to do XYZ because . . ."
- "I decided to . . ."
- "I married him . . ."

Here are some further observations.

- You notice that this person has a tendency to
  choose words that reflect their own agency,
  volition, and choice. Totally indicative of an
  internal reference!
- What's more, you suspect they may be more
  oriented toward options than they are to
  procedures because they tend to focus on the
  available possibilities and what they
  personally wish to do with those options.
- You notice loads of "I" statements (for example,
  this person doesn't say "we got married" or "he

married me," but "*I* married *him*"), showing you that they have an internal, individual focus.

- Finally, you notice how all of this is delivered in a tone of voice that is quiet, high pitched, and rapid. Sentences are long and complex but rushed, without you being able to get a word in.

Are you beginning to get a richer sense of who this person is?

You might hypothesize that this person is dominant, a little self-absorbed, and highly energetic, but that at their core, they are slightly insecure and in a rush to prove something.

Luckily for you, you can build on this hypothesis with every conversation, and with focused listening and careful inference-making, you can begin to see deeply inside this person's head, developing an understanding of things they themselves might not even be aware of!

But you don't have to do all this guesswork in the dark. There is one very obvious way to directly test and refine your hypotheses, and that's to ask questions. We'll be looking at questions in the next and final chapter.

Summary:

- People think in verbs and nouns with other parts of speech added after the fact. These additional word choices reveal a lot about a person and can be considered "Word Clues."

Pay attention to adverb use and the story they tell about how the person sees themselves and others. Notice what is emphasized, what is ignored, and especially pay attention to recurring patterns of words.

- Tone of voice is a part of body language and may be one of the most meaningful components of what a person is communicating. Notice breath (speed and depth), volume, articulation (clarity of speech, enunciation), speaking speed, and voice pitch.

- "Function words" (such as pronouns, articles, prepositions, conjunctions, and auxiliary verbs) give more important clues to a person's mindset than "content words" (nouns, adjectives, verbs, adverbs). They tell you about the way the speaker understands relationships, objects, and the world in general, as well as all about their emotional state, personality, age, and social class. High personal pronoun use suggests a focus on the self, liars tend to focus on "we" while avoiding personal pronouns, and heavy article use (a, the) suggests a concrete thinking style.

- There is significant overlap in Word Clues, tone of voice, function words, and the meta-program a person is running. Listen carefully for words that signal things like internal or external frame of reference, necessity- or possibility-focused thinking, or matching versus mismatching focus.

Chapter 12: The Art of Asking the Right Questions

You can tell a lot about somebody by reading:

- Their body language
- Their clothing
- Their voice
- Their posture
- Their accent
- Their gait
- The words they use
- The words they *don't* use
- Their facial expressions…

But at some point, you're going to need to go a little deeper and get more detailed information. And sometimes, the only way to get that information is to come out and ask.

There are a million questions we could ask.

So what's the best question?

Often, it's the one that get us the information we want... while appearing on the surface to be completely unrelated.

Let's take a closer look at how to ask questions that really help you learn the most you can about people.

<u>*The Kipling Method*</u>

5W1H is a way to ask questions and solve problems, and is meant to help you see ideas and problems from different points of view.

It helps you get to the bottom of a problem and figure out how to fix it. It's pretty straightforward.

The acronym stands for:

- What
- Where
- When
- Why
- Who
- How

5W1H is also called the Kipling method after the British author and poet Rudyard Kipling, who came up with the idea. Kipling used five W questions in his poem "The Elephant's Child," which is the story of an extremely curious elephant who is interested in everything around him.

It may sound obvious, but when reading and analyzing people, we can use the Kipling method to help us structure our efforts to gather information that will help us understand them better.

What

We often ask "what" to seek things that are and will be. We can use this when we are interested in knowing something specific about a person.

Examples:

- What do you intend to do?
- What do you enjoy doing?
- What pisses you off?

Where

"Where" tries to locate an action or event in three-dimensional space. This can be a simple space, such as on, above, under, or below, or something like a country, a building, a type of location, or even a vague context or environment. When a person answers this kind of question, they are giving you valuable information about how they contextualize and locate certain ideas.

Examples:

- Where did you get that bubbly personality?
- Where did you study?
- Where is this relationship going?

When

"When" looks for a place in time and can mean two different things—either a point in time that has passed, or one that might still come.

Examples:

- When will you be finished?
- When should we meet?
- When did you give me the money?

Why

When you ask "why," you are looking for links between causes and effects. This question word probes for a far more sophisticated depth of understanding. Knowing what someone has done doesn't always give you insight into their reasons and motivations.

But if you know *why* people have done something, you can begin to understand the world of meaning they have constructed for themselves in their own heads.

Examples:

- Why did you do that?
- Why did that happen?
- Why is it important for us to try it again?

Who

"Who" brings people into the picture and links them to actions and things. It's a question that directly asks about the relational human aspects to any situation. The most interesting people in any scenario tend to be the ones who are causing an action, or else deriving a benefit or penalty from that action.

Examples:

- Who is this work for?
- Who will benefit most from what you propose?
- Who else would be interested?

How

"How" is a question that asks for "verbs of process." In other words, the answer is usually an adverb. Knowing what we know about how adverbs are almost always powerful Word Clues, we can ask how to dig deeper into what has happened or what will happen.

Examples:

- How did you do that?
- How did you get everybody's attention?
- How are you finding this project?

Though the above might seem elementary, we can sometimes forget that the questions we ask play a major role in the type of information we're likely to extract from someone.

> **Example:** Let's imagine that we're talking to the woman we introduced in the previous section—the one who says, "I married him" rather than "He married me." Let's say that, given all your observations, you make a hypothesis about her motivation as a person: You guess that she is very goal-oriented and independent.
>
> So, you ask her some questions and notice that almost all of her answers begin with "I think" or "I feel." When you ask a *how* question, she answers with statements about how she achieved something, what she wanted, what she chose, and what she thought of the outcome.
>
> When you ask her a *why* question, you notice that she doesn't attribute many outcomes to random chance or the actions of others, but rather to her own actions. Incidentally, you also notice that she appears to quite enjoy being asked questions of this kind and is happy to talk about herself . . .

Bit by bit, your questions mine data that you use to strengthen and refine the working model you have of her. All questions will yield interesting information, but *why* and *how* questions tend to be more open-ended and invite more colorful responses. These are the ones most likely to give you an insight into how a person thinks.

On the other hand, pay attention to the kind of questions the person is asking you. When you bear in mind that it's recurrent patterns that matter and never just a single question, it's obvious that a person's question shows you what they're most interested in.

- **Who?** This is a person who is interested in relationships and people.
- **What?** The details matter to them.
- **Where, when?** They have a more procedural view and want to construct a narrative in a time and place.
- **Why?** This person is interested in cause and effect, motivations, meaning, and bigger-picture ideas.
- **How?** As above, but the person is asking for more explanation, detail, and nuance.

The questions a person chooses to ask can tell you what they see as the most important element of a situation. For example:

A: "I got a C minus in math again."
B: "What?! Who is your teacher?"

Assumptive Questions

Imagine there is an ad in a beauty magazine. The ad copy says:

> *"Stop wasting money on harsh drying toners"* and *"We love simplicity as much as you do."*

The ad has made certain forceful assumptions, namely:

- That you are the kind of person who knows what toner is.
- That you actually use toner and spend money on it.
- That you're dissatisfied with both the expense and harshness of toners.
- That you love simplicity.

While marketers use assumptions like this to artificially create the kind of consumer they want for their product, and generate the sort of desire that results in profit, the same technique can be used to confirm your own hypotheses about people and to sneakily *pose a statement as a question.*

Consider these examples, which all *look* like questions, but aren't.

In order to answer them, you have to accept the hidden assumption within:

- How much do you care? (Assumption: You do care.)
- How will you persuade her? (Assumption: You want to persuade her and are going to do it, it's possible to persuade her in the first place, and perhaps there are many different ways to do it.)
- Where do you buy your cheese? (Assumption: You buy cheese!)
- What are you avoiding admitting to yourself? (Assumption: There is something you are avoiding, you know what it is, and the person asking the question is entitled to be told all about it.)

Simply by framing a question a certain way, we are implying something about the possibilities for the form the answer will take. The way the other person chooses to respond to these implications can speak volumes.

> **Example:** Let's imagine you ask the woman in our example, "So what do you think your biggest flaws are?" and you notice that she can't quite answer the question, or says something like, "I guess people can find my confidence a little intimidating…"

This tells you that the hidden assumption (i.e., that she has flaws) is actually not something she acknowledges—that it is not part of her mental model. But if you had asked outright, "Are you a little arrogant?" you would not have received such a revealing answer!

On the other hand, the questions that people ask *you* can also reveal their own assumptions, biases, and preconceptions.

> **Example:** Someone asks, "So, was his proposal really romantic?"

They are not just assuming that there *was* a proposal, they're conveying a whole world of value judgments and expectations. They are asking you about the thing that *they* are focused on and value.

Even though they are asking the questions and you are answering, you are actually gleaning information about their values, priorities, and meta-programs! Consider this exchange and see what the question implies about the asker's values and frame of reference:

A: "I've gone vegan. It's been six months now!"
B: "Oh my God, good on you! Tell me, how much weight have you lost? Do you find your skin is much clearer?"

Chunking Up and Chunking Down

"Chunking" = putting together or breaking up information or data into bigger or smaller pieces.

In conversation, chunking is a way to ask questions or organize ideas so as to reach an agreement or gain clarification. But the way that people use chunking in their own speech can tell you interesting things about them as people—if you pay attention!

- **"Chunking up"** is when you move from specific and detailed information to more general or abstract information.
  - How and why questions tend to lead to chunking up.
- **"Chunking down"** goes the other way and happens whenever we move from broad generalizations and abstractions down to finer specifics.
  - Where, what, when, and who questions tend to lead to chunking down.

When you chunk up, it is as though you are zooming out of the conversation to gain a broad, top-down overview of it, or as though you were getting a larger and more general "map" of the conversation terrain.

When you chunk down, it's like taking a deep dive or getting stuck back into the nitty-gritty level, filling in the inevitable gaps you have on a more abstract overview.

Understanding how chunking works can help you in three ways:

1. It can help you structure your own questions so that you zoom in and out of the topic appropriately, helping you gain a broad yet detailed understanding of what the other person is trying to share with you.
2. It can help you understand how the other person is using chunking, and what this implies about how they're structuring their own mental maps.
3. It can help you identify differences in chunking styles—typically, misunderstandings and conflicts arise from a mismatch of chunking styles. Making sure that chunking styles are balanced and aligned can smooth over conversational difficulties.

So how do you use chunking in a conversation where you're trying to learn more about a person?

First, chunking up questions will help you zoom out and find commonality, look for themes, or help you summarize what you've been told so you can reflect it, showing that you understand and are paying attention.

Example:
A: "So after we lived in Puerto Rico for a while, we found ourselves back in Italy, but within just two months, because of work, we found ourselves pulling the kids out of school again and doing a year-long stint in France. We wanted to come back to Puerto Rico, but... oh well, long story short, we're here in New Zealand instead!"

B: "Wow, what a whirlwind! So overall you moved, what, four times in one year?!"

A: "Pretty much."

B: "What toll do you think all that had on you?"

A: "Well, it was hard, but we all learned a lot, I will say that."

Speaker B above has asked two chunking up questions:

- The first ("You moved four times?") more or less summarizes the key theme of the story ("a whirlwind!")
- The second ("what was the toll on you?") probes a little for bigger overarching themes that connect all these disparate travel experiences. The question itself is looking for a broader, more abstract analysis, rather than further details about what happened in each

particular country, or the exact dates they went there.

If Speaker B continues asking these kinds of chunking up questions, eventually the pair might find themselves having a very detached and abstracted conversation, indeed, about how humankind has always been nomadic, the resilience of children, globalization, the philosophical and political implications of being dislocated from the land, etc.

If A and B are enjoying this, it *may* be a good conversation, but it probably won't be a conversation in which they learn much about one another as people!

Adding some chunking down questions will not only make for a more balanced and comfortable conversation, it will also allow more personal and detailed information to come through.

The devil is in the details, but so are people's more interesting idiosyncrasies!

➜ **A good rule of thumb:** Stick to no more than three questions of one type in a row.

If you ask three chunking up questions, switch to a chunking down question to drill down a little more deeply into a specific idea or detail. But don't stay there too long or you'll risk getting "caught in the weeds." Come up for air after a few chunking down questions to get a breather and a bird's-eye view:

B: "What toll do you think all that had on you?"

A: "Well, it was hard, but we all learned a lot, I will say that."

B: "So be honest, which country was your favorite?"

A: "Hm... honestly? I thought I'd love France, but it was nothing like I'd imagined. I'm really loving New Zealand, which I never expected to."

B: "What surprised you most about France?"

You can almost imagine zooming in on the mental map, from countries → favorite countries → France → something specific about France.
But if Speaker A had said, "You know what, they all drink too much!" and Speaker B had another fifty questions about what kind of wine, the conversation would not only stall, but they'd stop gaining further insight into Speaker A.

Here are some examples of chunking-up-style questions (importantly, these are not necessarily verbatim):

- What do you think that means?
- Why did that happen?
- So in the bigger picture...?
- Is that connected to...?
- What do you think that says about...?
- How do all these things connect?
- What do you think of...?
- How do you make sense of...?

Here are some examples of chunking-down-style questions:

- How did you like that?
- What happened?
- What happened next?
- When...?
- Who did that?
- Tell me more about...

If you make sure to balance the *ratio* of chunking up and chunking down questions in any conversation, you'll likely keep things moving along at an enjoyable and balanced pace.

But remember to pay attention to learn more about your conversation partner.

Do they continually ask chunking up questions themselves and respond most enthusiastically to chunking up questions from you?

This could mean a few things:

- Organizing, analytical, and pattern-seeking questions typically show intelligence, awareness, and mastery of a topic.
- This pattern can also hint at a desire to be personally and emotionally distant from a certain topic.

If you're having a heated conversation with someone and they suddenly seem to retreat into lofty abstractions about nobody in particular, ask whether you've struck a nerve and if chunking up is serving as an evasive maneuver.

Do they continually ask chunking down questions or respond most enthusiastically to yours?

This could indicate a narrow, focused, or even enthusiastic sense of attention to concrete matters, but it can also signal a lack of insight and critical thinking. People who are most comfortable continually chunking down might be:

- Running the procedural meta-program.
- Bored or lost in a conversation that doesn't anchor directly onto something in their literal lives in that moment.
- Signaling that they are interested not in the topic at hand, but in *you*. You'll notice that people who flirt, for example, are seldom having a deep and meaningful conversation!

Finally, if you do notice that someone prefers chunking down, pay attention to the kind of questions they ask to gain insight into what they're primarily focused on.

- Are they more interested in people, places, what happened, the prices of things, family connections, the sequence of events?
- If you're talking very generally, notice what triggers people to dive deeper into detail.
- They are communicating what inspires and excites them. By the same token, someone who repeatedly chunks up while you're trying to

chunk down might be telling you that they don't find that particular topic very interesting!

You may be wondering if every question is potentially a chunking up or chunking down question.

The answer is yes!

That said, there are also questions you could ask that act to keep the conversation at more or less the same level of depth—i.e., they neither chunk up or down but stay at that level of focus.

At the end of the day, it's not any particular question itself that will yield greater or lesser insight into someone's character.

Rather, it's *how* that question is used.

This is why it's important to create hypotheses in your mind to explain your perceptions and observations. That way, you "test" that observation through targeted questions. At the same time, you listen to *their* questions, what they are probing for, what they are focusing on, and what that tells you about their motivations, priorities, and thinking style.

We've discussed a few methods so far:

- Listening for Word Clues
- Identifying meta-programs
- Noticing overall language use

But each of these is relatively weak on its own. When combined, they become incredibly powerful.

Have you ever heard people say that they've spoken to someone for hours, or even known them for years, and yet they know nothing about them? That's because their conversation lacked strategy and focus.

With a little practice and awareness, though, you can be the opposite—you will be able to talk to people for an astonishingly short amount of time, yet see more clearly into the depths of who they are as a person.

Here are a few last hints and tips for asking questions that will help you fine-tune your people-reading skills:

- As a rule, begin with open-ended questions and lead to more closed ones once the flow of conversation is established.
  - This neatly maps on to the habit of asking more chunking up questions first, and then after you've gained an overview (and the person is more comfortable with you), you can drill a little deeper with a closed question that probes for a specific, detailed answer.
- Be careful not to ask too many questions (of any kind). It will feel like an interview or interrogation, and the person will definitely register that the exchange of information is imbalanced.

- Try posing some questions as statements—for example, "You're one of those super smart people, so I bet you learned all sorts of amazing things while living there."
  o Such statements act as questions since they spur conversation and inspire the other person to tell you what you want to know. Extra points if you can be a little unexpected or controversial—the way people jump in to respond tells you a lot about where they are psychologically: "Smart!? Well, I certainly didn't feel that way at the time. Quite the opposite, actually . . ."

Finally, one final tip is to work on the delivery of questions.

When you ask:

- Use a friendly, relaxed tone of voice.
- Don't use eye contact.
- Only once you've asked the question, pause and then make eye contact—this body language acts like a nonverbal invitation for them to speak, and communicates your respectful interest in their answer, without being pushy.

Finally, pay attention to *their* eye contact. Avoiding your gaze or looking away may suggest their desire to avoid that question!

Summary:

- A great way to get information about a person is to ask targeted questions. The best questions are those that appear on the surface to be asking about something unrelated.
- We can use the Kipling method (5W1H—who, what, where, when, why, and how) to help us structure our efforts to gather information that will help us understand a person better.
- An assumptive question is one that forces certain assumptions and thus implies something about the form the answer could take. The way someone responds to these implications can speak volumes, so notice what they focus on and what they dismiss.
- The questions that people ask *you* can also reveal their own assumptions, biases, and preconceptions.
- "Chunking" is the way information is grouped into bigger or smaller pieces. The way people use chunking in their own speech or respond to your chunking can tell you interesting things about them.
- "Chunking up" is moving from specific and detailed information to more general or abstract information and can signal detachment or critical thinking, while "chunking down" inquires about details and specifics and can signal interest or more concrete thinking. Notice the person's chunking style and how they respond to yours.
- Keep questions open-ended and varied and don't ask too many. Try to pose some questions as statements and note the response. Ask with a friendly tone and use appropriate eye contact, leaving enough space for an answer.

Soft probing means using low-stakes testing to verify your theories and hypotheses about someone right there, as you interact with them. The SUE framework lets you listen for revealing discrepancies and continuously test your baseline hypothesis. Beware of behavioral confirmation and don't "lead" people.